Penguin

THE HOUSES OF WE

THE HOUSES OF NORMANDY, BLOIS AND ANJOU

THE HOUSE OF PLANTAGENET

THE HOUSES OF LANCASTER AND YORK

* Now in paperback

THE HOUSE OF TUDOR

Henry VII	Sean Cunningham
Henry VIII*	John Guy
Edward VI*	Stephen Alford
Mary I*	John Edwards
Elizabeth I	Helen Castor

THE HOUSE OF STUART

James I	Thomas Cogswell
Charles I*	Mark Kishlansky
[Cromwell*	David Horspool]
Charles II*	Clare Jackson
James II	David Womersley
William III & Mary II*	Jonathan Keates
Anne	Richard Hewlings

THE HOUSE OF HANOVER

George I	Tim Blanning
George II	Norman Davies
George III	Jeremy Black
George IV	Stella Tillyard
William IV	Roger Knight
Victoria*	Jane Ridley

THE HOUSES OF SAXE-COBURG & GOTHA AND WINDSOR

Edward VII*	Richard Davenport-Hines
George V*	David Cannadine
Edward VIII*	Piers Brendon
George VI*	Philip Ziegler
Elizabeth II*	Douglas Hurd

* Now in paperback

NORMAN DAVIES

George II
Not Just a British Monarch

ALLEN LANE
an imprint of
PENGUIN BOOKS

ALLEN LANE

UK | USA | Canada | Ireland | Australia
India | New Zealand | South Africa

Allen Lane is part of the Penguin Random House group of companies
whose addresses can be found at global.penguinrandomhouse.com

Penguin
Random House
UK

First published 2021
001

Copyright © Norman Davies, 2021

The moral right of the author has been asserted

Set in 9.5/13.5 pt Sabon LT Std
Typeset by Jouve (UK), Milton Keynes
Printed and bound in Great Britain by Clays Ltd, Elcograf S.p.A.

The authorized representative in the EEA is Penguin Random House Ireland,
Morrison Chambers, 32 Nassau Street, Dublin D02 YH68

A CIP catalogue record for this book is available from the British Library

ISBN: 978-0-141-97842-0

www.greenpenguin.co.uk

MIX
Paper from
responsible sources
FSC® C018179

Penguin Random House is committed to a
sustainable future for our business, our readers
and our planet. This book is made from Forest
Stewardship Council® certified paper.

Contents

Prologue

Georg Ludwig, the old *Kurfürst* or 'Duke and Prince-elector' of Braunschweig-Lüneburg – Georges-Louis, as he thought of himself – died on the morning of 11 June 1727, aged sixty-seven, in the Bishop's Palace at Osnabrück, in the very room where he had been born. Two days earlier, travelling home from his latest foreign trip, he had supped and slept in a Dutch inn at Delden, the last township of the United Provinces before the Imperial frontier. The next day, rising at dawn, he stepped into his carriage at 7.30 a.m., accompanied only by Hardenberg, his court marshal, and by Fabrice, his domestic *Kammerherr* or 'equerry'. They would report that he had looked well and was eager to press on. After ten miles or so, they bade farewell to their Dutch cavalry escort and crossed into the Holy Roman Empire.

The duke-elector was undoubtedly weary – worn out not just by the discomforts of travel but equally by the accumulated stress of decades in high office, by the lengthy and scandalous rift with his deceased wife, and by endless quarrels with his only son, Georg August. According to later rumours, he had also taken fright at a letter written by his late and long-alienated wife, which had somehow been handed to him at Delden and had prophesied his death within a twelve-month. Yet, as his biographer emphasizes, he appeared to be 'in good health' and 'good humour', and to have 'much to look forward to'. He was aiming to stop in the nearby town of Osnabrück before heading out on the last, eighty-mile stage of his journey to his summer residence:

> At Osnabrück he would meet [his brother] Ernst August [the prince-bishop], the last relative of his own generation since their half-sister, Sophia Charlotte, had died in 1725 ... The prince-bishop was to join [him and his mistress] Melusine [von der Schulenberg] for the whole visit. At Herrenhausen George would see Anna Louisa [the love child of his liaison with Melusine] settled in the Delitzsche Palais. Best of all, his daughter, the queen of Prussia, would travel from Berlin to Herrenhausen, where the double-marriage plan [for his grand-children] would be finalized. Now that the shadows of war were dispelled he had told his daughter that this was the time for a public announcement ... Quite apart from meeting relatives, George looked forward to seeing what progress had been made at Herrenhausen with his latest project there; it was only in 1725 that he had ordered the planting of the linden trees that were to form a long, double allée between the summer residence and the nearby town.[1]

Then, somewhere in the vicinity of the hamlet of Nordhorn, Georg Ludwig suddenly ordered the carriage to halt, and descended for a break. When he returned to his companions, they saw with horror that his face was badly twisted and that he was unable to speak. He had suffered a stroke. A physician was called up from the line of following vehicles, and the decision taken to rush the stricken man over the remaining twenty-five miles of bumpy road to Osnabrück. Once there, the comatose patient was carried up the back stairs of the palace into the familiar room.

For twenty-four hours, the duke lay fully dressed on a couch, only regaining consciousness briefly to raise his hat in silence, as if to greet the circle of anxious courtiers. As they watched, his eyes closed and his breathing slowed until it became imperceptible. Soon after the second midnight, Melusine approached him in the candlelight, examining his lips through a magnifying glass for signs of moisture. She declared that he had expired. The alarm was raised. Under the guidance of the prince-bishop, arrangements were promptly made: firstly to convey the body of the deceased to the family's principal seat at the Leineschloss, to prepare for the funeral, and secondly to send express news by courier to the dead duke's son and heir. By custom and belief, and with no dissent, the forty-four-year-old Georg August was deemed to have acceded instantaneously to all his father's many lands and titles: *Seine Hoheit, Herzog* (Duke) of Calenberg, Lüneburg, Grubenhagen, Celle, Lauenberg etc.; *Erzschatzmeister* (Arch-treasurer) and *Fürst* (Prince-elector) of the Holy Roman Empire; *Erzpannerherr* (Arch-banner-bearer) of Osnabrück's episcopal *Hochstift*; *Seine Durchlaucht Kurfürst* of Braunschweig-Lüneburg, and, 'By the Grace of God' (in the family's preferred form), *Sa majesté, Défenseur de la Foi, Roi de la Grande Bretagne, France et Irlande.*

Note on Linguistic Transpositions

For practical purposes, every historical narrative has to be written in a single language. One may write a history of the kings of England in English, or in Welsh or in Algonquin, but not, without serious confusion, in several languages simultaneously. A volume describing each of the English or British monarchs in their native languages would start with a chapter in Anglo-Saxon, followed by chapters in Danish, Norman French, Middle English, Tudor and Stuart English, Lallands, Dutch, French and German.

Yet every monolingual narrative, when applied to subjects with a multilingual or multicultural context, inevitably does injury to reality. A historical account written exclusively in English but applied to a non-English or partly English theme is in danger of misrepresenting it; attempts made to anglicize all the relevant names, places, titles and key terms without reference to the originals are misguided.

In the present case, the monarch in question was born and bred in Germany to a French-speaking aristocratic family; he came to the throne of his English-speaking kingdoms in middle age. Furthermore, as a prince of the Holy Roman Empire, he always retained an active role in German affairs. In consequence, his whole reign and persona were characterized by a linguistic triality which historians should somehow endeavour to reflect. The essential colour and tone of his life are undermined by the exclusive use of Anglocentric terminology.

The monarch's title, for example, conveys a powerful and constantly repeated message about who and what he was. Yet almost all the books about him are content to call him 'king' – King George II, successor to King George I and predecessor to King George III. This convention, borne on the cover of this volume only for the sake of series uniformity, hardly does him justice. Apart from being king three times over, he was, as we have noted, *Herzog* (Duke) of Braunschweig-Lüneburg and *Kurfürst* (Prince-elector) of the Holy Roman Empire. At the risk of some initial confusion, therefore, historians and biographers should try to find a way of indicating the true complexities. They cannot possibly use all his titles all the time. But they *can* use an amalgam of the two most important ones, calling him 'king-elector' instead of 'king'. Such amalgams are not unknown. Victoria, Queen of the United Kingdom, was also 'Empress of India', and was frequently referred to as the 'empress-queen' or 'queen-empress'.

Next comes the name of the king-elector's dynasty. For the last 300 years, English-speakers have grown accustomed to the artificial formula of the 'house of Hanover'. Few are aware that this designation was invented in England in 1701 for the purposes of the Act of Settlement. And inaccuracies abound. The *Oxford English Dictionary*, no less, states complacently that 'the Elector of Hanover in

1714 became the King of England' – which is doubly inaccurate. The princely family which the British were taught to call the 'Hanoverians' knew themselves to be members of the 'house of Welf', or Guelph, or more precisely of the Welfs of Braunschweig-Lüneburg; and the change to their new-fangled name must have caused them some consternation. For it was not unimportant in the subtle process of image-making. The group of Protestant fundamentalists, headed by King William III, who coined the ingenious 'Hanoverian' formula undoubtedly avoided the Guelph label because of its strong Catholic associations.

So what are historians supposed to do? Do they connive with the sleight of hand which pulled the so-called 'Hanoverians' out of the hat in 1701, or do they look for a more equitable solution? Writing in English, they can sensibly refer to the well-established 'Brunswick' in place of the super-Germanic Braunschweig, producing a reasonable compromise in 'Brunswick-Lüneburg'. They might also think of referring to the dynasty as 'Hanoverians' in the context of their insular realms, while retaining the original name in relation to the continental ones. Here, alas, they would run into objections from Wolfenbüttel, and would be pushed into adopting a monstrous package such as 'the Guelphs from the Calenberg-Lüneburg line of Brunswick-Lüneburg'. In the present text, therefore, the king-elector is variously presented as head of the 'Calenberg Guelphs' or 'Hanoverian Guelphs'.

Equally, it is no simple matter to find a suitable name for the complex entity made up by the dynasty's multiple realms. The Hanoverian Guelphs sought to weld the Kingdoms of Great

Britain and Ireland and the Electorate of Brunswick-Lüneburg into one hybrid whole, ruled in personal union by one and the same sovereign. (Their claim to the kingship of France was no more than symbolic.) But a composite name such as 'Great Britain-Ireland-Brunswick-Lüneburg' makes a clumsy mouthful, and some form of shorthand is clearly required. Despite the risks, it is not too impossible to subsume the Kingdom of Ireland under the general heading of 'Great Britain', and not too outrageous to subsume the dependent territories of Lauenburg, Bremen and Verden, and Bentheim under the heading of the Electorate. Moreover, though the Electorate did not formally adopt the Hanover name until 1814, on its elevation to a kingdom, the colloquial term of *Kurfürstentum Hannover* was indeed coming into general circulation in the eighteenth century. So the artificial hybrid of Great Britain-Hanover is less unacceptable than other alternatives.

Yet that is not the end of it. The historian has still to decide what to call the man who mounted his royal and electoral thrones in June 1727. In one part of those realms, he was crowned as 'George'; in the other he was Georg August and Georgius Augustus. Were it not for the ambiguation caused by the eighth month of the year, one might adopt the half-English and half-German form of George August. In which case, the eminently appropriate appellation of 'King-elector George II Augustus' seems the best solution.

Finally, it is a common practice in popular English-language history books, especially in the USA, to translate all foreign words and sentences, thereby losing much of the flavour. The best-known quotation attributed to George II

Augustus derives from the day when his dying wife urged him to remarry after her death. 'Oh no,' the monarch is universally reported as saying, 'I shall have mistresses.'[1] But that, of course, is *not* what he actually said.

The Hanoverian Guelphs

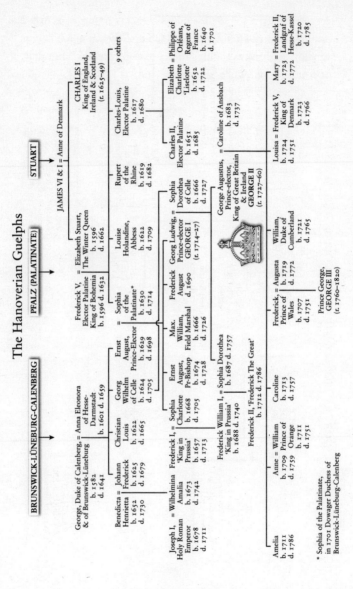

STUART

JAMES VI & I = Anne of Denmark

CHARLES I, King of England, Ireland & Scotland (r. 1625–49)

9 others

Charles-Louis, Elector Palatine b. 1617 d. 1680

Elizabeth = Philippe of Orléans, Charlotte Regent of 'Liselotte' France b. 1652 b. 1640 d. 1722 d. 1701

PFALZ (PALATINATE)

Frederick V, Elector Palatine King of Bohemia b. 1596 d. 1632

= Elizabeth Stuart, The Winter Queen b. 1596 d. 1662

Rupert of the Rhine b. 1619 d. 1682

Louise Holandine, Abbess b. 1622 d. 1709

Sophia of the Palatinate* b. 1630 d. 1714

Charles II, Elector Palatine b. 1651 d. 1685

= Caroline of Ansbach b. 1683 d. 1737

BRUNSWICK-LÜNEBURG-CALENBERG

George, Duke of Calenberg & of Brunswick-Lüneburg b. 1582 d. 1641

= Anna Eleonora of Hesse-Darmstadt b. 1601 d. 1659

Christian Louis b. 1622 d. 1665

Georg Wilhelm of Celle b. 1624 d. 1705

Ernst August, Prince-Elector b. 1629 d. 1698

Johann Frederick b. 1625 d. 1679

Benedicta Henrietta b. 1652 d. 1730

Ernst August, Pr-Bishop b. 1674 d. 1728

Max. William, Field Marshal b. 1666 d. 1726

Frederick August b. 1690 d. 1714

Georg Ludwig, Prince-elector GEORGE I (r. 1714–27) = Sophia Dorothea of Celle b. 1666 d. 1727

George Augustus, Prince-elector, King of Great Britain & Ireland GEORGE II (r. 1727–60)

Frederick I, 'King in Prussia' b. 1657 d. 1713 = Sophia Charlotte b. 1668 d. 1705

Ernst August, Pr-Bishop b. 1674 d. 1728

Joseph I, Holy Roman Emperor b. 1678 d. 1711 = Wilhelmina Amalia b. 1673 d. 1742

Frederick William I, 'King in Prussia' b. 1688 d. 1740 = Sophia Dorothea b. 1687 d. 1757

Frederick II, 'Frederick The Great' b. 1712 d. 1786

William, Duke of Cumberland b. 1721 d. 1765

Louisa = Frederick V, King of Denmark b. 1724 b. 1723 d. 1751 d. 1766

Mary = Frederick II, Landgraf of Hesse-Kassel b. 1723 b. 1720 d. 1772 d. 1785

Frederick, Prince of Wales b. 1707 d. 1751 = Augusta b. 1719 d. 1772

Prince George, GEORGE III (r. 1760–1820)

Amelia b. 1711 d. 1786

Anne = William b. 1709 Prince of d. 1759 Orange b. 1711 d. 1751

Caroline b. 1713 d. 1757

* Sophia of the Palatinate, in 1701 Dowager Duchess of Brunswick-Lüneburg-Calenberg

NORTH EUROPEAN DYNASTIES ACQUIRING ROYAL STATUS

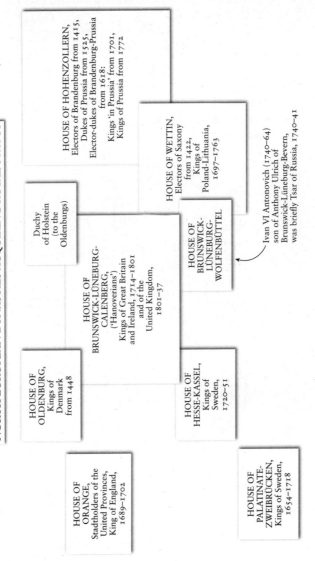

HOUSE OF HOHENZOLLERN,
Electors of Brandenburg from 1415,
Dukes of Prussia from 1525,
Elector-dukes of Brandenburg-Prussia
from 1618:
Kings 'in Prussia' from 1701,
Kings of Prussia from 1772

HOUSE OF WETTIN,
Electors of Saxony
from 1422,
Kings of
Poland-Lithuania,
1697–1763

Duchy
of Holstein
(to the
Oldenburgs)

HOUSE OF
BRUNSWICK-
LÜNEBURG-
WOLFENBÜTTEL

Ivan VI Antonovich (1740–64)
son of Anthony Ulrich of
Brunswick-Lüneburg-Bevern,
was briefly Tsar of Russia, 1740–41

HOUSE OF
BRUNSWICK-LÜNEBURG-
CALENBERG,
('Hanoverians')
Kings of Great Britain
and Ireland, 1714–1801
and of the
United Kingdom,
1801–37

HOUSE OF OLDENBURG,
Kings of
Denmark
from 1448

HOUSE OF HESSE-KASSEL,
Kings of
Sweden,
1720–51

HOUSE OF ORANGE,
Stadtholders of the
United Provinces,
King of England,
1689–1702

HOUSE OF PALATINATE-
ZWEIBRÜCKEN,
Kings of Sweden,
1654–1718

N

0   100 miles

0   200 km

×Culloden (1746)

(North
Britain)

Edinburgh
×Prestonpans (1745)

North Sea

KINGDOM OF GREAT BRITAIN

KINGDOM
OF
IRELAND

•**Dublin**

Liverpool•

Derby•

(England and Wales)

Harwich•

London •

Bristol•

Portsmouth•

English Channel

*ATLANTIC
OCEAN*

St Helier•

FRANCE

The British Isles *c.*1750

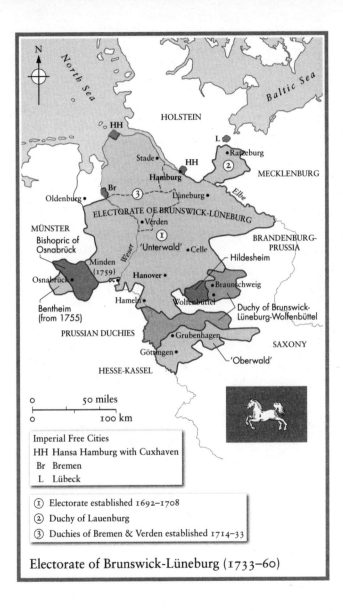

Electorate of Brunswick-Lüneburg (1733–60)

George II Augustus

I
1683: The World of George Augustus von Welf

George Augustus was born on 10 November 1683 in the family home, the Leineschloss, in Old Hanover. Grandson of the reigning Duke of Calenberg, and son of the heir apparent, Georg Ludwig, he grew up under the formative influences of his grandparents, Duke Ernst August (1629–98) and Duchess Sophie von der Pfalz (1630–1714). They usually spoke French among themselves and German to God and their servants.

Any relative or retainer asked about the infant's identity would have replied a 'prince of Brunswick'. They might have added that the ancient Imperial county of Brunswick had long been divided between the senior line of Brunswick-Lüneburg-Wolfenbüttel and the junior line of Brunswick-Lüneburg-Calenberg, both of which, confusingly, used the same shortened title. 'Don't worry,' the informant might have said, 'they are all Protestant Guelphs, and are always carving up and redistributing their estates.'

Even though the Calenbergs' *Residenz* lay in Hanover, the adjective 'Hanoverian' never applied to them. Landed aristocrats identified with their ancestral lands, not with cities. To them, the 'house of Hanover' would have sounded as odd as an English king accredited to a 'house of London'. In 1683, the 'Hanoverian idea' had still to be invented.

George Augustus – *recte* Georg August von Welf, to use his surname – belonged to an ancient European clan, the house of Guelph made famous by the medieval wars of Guelphs and Ghibellines. They traced their ancestry to a fifth-century associate of Attila the Hun. The paternal line descended from Otto the Child (1204–52), the first Duke of Brunswick-Lüneburg.[1]

In the seventeenth century, the house of Guelph was split by contending religious allegiances. The clan's Catholic branches included the d'Este lords of Ferrara, destined to mingle with the Habsburgs. The Protestant Guelphs, who had turned Lutheran at the Reformation, were crowded into a dozen North German states, and had intermarried with ruling families from Sweden to Prussia.

Duke Ernst August and his brothers had long been laying the foundations of a mini-state. After the Thirty Years War, though still vassals of the Holy Roman Empire, they had followed the princely fashion and had acquired quasi-sovereign status. Their father, the first Duke of Calenberg, had bequeathed them a clutch of territories in the Weser Valley separated into two main districts – the *Unterwald* round Calenberg and Hanover, and the *Oberwald* round Göttingen. (The Wolfenbüttel Guelphs owned the intervening land.) The Grubenhagen district was added in 1665, Lauenberg twenty years later.

By 1683, only two of the four brothers were still alive. The elder one, Georg Wilhelm (1624–1705), a comrade-in-arms of William of Orange and often known as the Duke of Zell

(Celle), had caused great complications by a morganatic marriage and by a long struggle to legitimize his only child, Sophia Dorothea. The younger one, Ernst August, by inheriting lands from his dead brothers, had assembled his own duchy, whose holdings were more substantial than their population of around 500,000 suggested. Valuable copper and iron mines, lying on the route to the seaports of Bremen and Hamburg, generated an income that supported a ducal army of 20,000–30,000 men.

The fortified city of Hamelin, twenty-seven miles from Hanover, augmented the duchy's military resources. Its fortress was a strategic bastion in the Empire's defences against the constant threat of French raids:

> Hamelin town's in Brunswick,
> By famous Hanover city.
> The River Weser broad and wide
> Washes its wall on the southern side.
> A prettier spot you'd never have spied . . .[2]

The geopolitical world of the Hanoverian Guelphs was bounded by the affairs of the Holy Roman Empire, which endured constant conflicts with France in the West and with the Ottomans in the East. In 1683, while the French invested Luxembourg, a vast Ottoman army laid siege to Vienna. To end that siege, the winged hussars of King John Sobieski of Poland charged down the Kahlenberg Hill to smash the sultan's camp and entered into legend. Georg Ludwig, an Imperial officer, witnessed the victory, and would certainly have told his son about it.[3]

'Kahlenberg', he might have explained, was not the same as 'Calenberg'.

The Empire's domestic affairs under the long-lived Emperor Leopold I (r. 1658–1705) were marked by the stagnating power of the Habsburgs and the waywardness of the princes, notably the Hohenzollerns. Princely rivalries were played out in the Imperial courts and diets, and in the politics of the nine Imperial Circles and of the *Reichsarmee*. The Imperial Diet met in Regensburg (Ratisbon). Frankfurt-am-Main hosted Imperial coronations. Brunswick-Lüneburg competed for power and influence with the twenty-eight member states of the Imperial Circle of Lower Saxony.[4]

Civilization was changing imperceptibly. The dominant political ideas of absolutism and the 'divine right of kings' were under attack from Spinoza and Locke. For the princes, the theory and practice of war were paramount; after the Battle of Rocroi in 1643, France had superseded Spain as Europe's leading military power. Economic ideas were still confined to the assumptions of mercantilism. The Empire's social structures were rigidly hierarchical, patriarchal and largely feudal. Religious conflicts were managed by the principle of *cuius regio, eius religio*: every prince determined his subjects' religion. The Scientific Revolution was gradually changing attitudes to religion; Isaac Newton's *Philosophae Naturalis Principia Mathematica* (1687) demonstrated that divine providence enjoyed no monopoly. In the arts, the Baroque emanated grandeur and exuberance; 1685 saw the birth near to Hanover of both Bach and Handel – one at Eisenach, the other at Halle.[5]

Any observer of the Holy Roman Empire could see that

the long-standing Habsburg ascendancy was built on a 'Dual Authority', where the emperors' position inside the Empire was perpetuated by their possession of extensive lands and military forces outside it. Leopold I, *Kaiser und König*, reigned simultaneously as elected emperor and hereditary King of Hungary. Now, in 1683, the Ottoman invasion of Hungary was putting the Dual Authority at risk. Leopold could only recover by calling for support on the Imperial princes and on allies such as the King of Poland. The Habsburgs' kingdom would be rescued by the Habsburgs' Empire, just as their position in the Empire had repeatedly been upheld by their extra-Imperial resources.

Such was the backdrop to the Leopoldine era's most remarkable development: the rise of Hohenzollern Prussia. Thirty years earlier, two lines of Hohenzollerns had been ruling two separate states – one the Imperial Electorate of Brandenburg and the other, 400 miles to the east, the duchy of Prussia. The Hohenzollern court in Berlin owed loyalty to the Habsburgs, its counterpart in Königsberg to the Kingdom of Poland. The elector and the duke, though kinsmen, had long ruled two different entities. In 1618, however, their inheritance was merged under one joint ruler, creating the dual state of Brandenburg-Prussia – one half still within the Empire, the other half outside it. Armed with their own version of Dual Authority, the Hohenzollerns would soon emulate the Habsburgs and embark on a strategic programme of aggrandizement, raising disloyalty to a fine art.

The ruler of Brandenburg-Prussia, who played his Dual Authority to perfection and was still active when George Augustus was born, was Duke-elector Frederick William von

Hohenzollern (r. 1640–88), usually known as 'the Great Elector'. Born in Berlin, he divided his early life between Königsberg and Warsaw, being both an Imperial prince and a Polish vassal. Familiar with the dual Polish-Lithuanian 'Commonwealth', once the largest state in Europe, he forged his independence by skilfully switching his loyalties; after 1675, having routed the previously invincible Swedish army at Fehrbellin, he openly aspired to mount a royal throne.[6]

Admiration for the 'Prussian gambit' was widespread. Yet one event was to give George Augustus an intimate insight into the Prussian mindset. In 1683, a daughter was born to the Great Elector-duke's kinsman, the Margrave of Brandenburg-Ansbach. Raised in Berlin alongside the Hohenzollerns' own grandchildren, Wilhelmine Karoline von Ansbach (1683–1737) was endowed with strong political antennae, and twenty-two years later was destined to marry George Augustus.

In the meantime, German princes lined up to acquire extra-Imperial titles, treading a path blazed by the dukes of Oldenburg, the Calenbergs' neighbours to the north-west, who had long occupied the throne of Denmark-Norway. The adolescent George Augustus began to see that several dynasties harboured similar royal ambitions. In 1697 the Calenbergs' eastern neighbour, August der Starke ('the Strong'), Duke-elector of Saxony, accepted election to the Polish throne.[7] In 1701, the Great Elector-duke's son, Frederick I, was crowned 'King in Prussia'. And in 1713, Victor Amadeus, Duke of Savoy, was raised by the Treaty of Utrecht to be sovereign King of Sicily.[8] Composite monarchies were multiplying fast. The young Calenberg prince could not have avoided the thought that his own family might one day benefit from the trend.

The Oldenburgs' affairs would have made a strong impression. Barely one day's ride from Hanover, Oldenburg had formed a Danish-ruled enclave within the Empire for two centuries. Despite generations in Copenhagen, its rulers spoke little Danish, and married into the same circle of high-born Protestant clans as the Calenbergs. The reigning king-duke, Christian V (r. 1670–99) was the son of George Augustus's great-aunt, Sophie Amelia of Brunswick-Lüneburg, and ruled over many distant territories, from Greenland to the North Cape. A firm Protestant and a principled absolutist, he spent much time warring with Sweden over supremacy in Scandinavia.[9] For their part, the Vasa kings of Sweden-Finland were juggling with their own collection of inherited territories, including two sizeable chunks of the Empire.[10] For young George Augustus, learning every day about the workings of monarchy, these complex configurations were the norm.

In the age of absolutism, when the authority of monarchs and dynasties was rarely questioned, dynastic Orders of Succession provided the foremost issue of international politics. Invariably complicated by religious affiliations, they overrode questions of national identity or economic interest, creating a constant source of conflict. In George Augustus's lifetime, they would spark a long series of major wars, from the Nine Years War of the Palatine Succession (1688–97) to that of the Austrian Succession (1740–48). The laws of succession, however, were not uniform. In much of Western Europe, including England, male primogeniture prevailed. In many German states, the ancient Salian Law excluded female inheritance altogether. And elsewhere, including Brunswick-Lüneburg, a dead ruler's inheritance was traditionally divided among his male offspring.

All ruling houses, therefore, dreading childlessness or the lack of male heirs, were often tempted to tamper with the rules. In 1682, Duke Ernst August had introduced primogeniture to Brunswick-Lüneburg-Calenberg by decree. In 1701, the ultra-Protestant William of Orange would arrange by Act of Parliament to exclude all Catholics from the English Succession, and in 1703 the Emperor-king Leopold's sons would sign a Mutual Pact of Succession to settle their differences. In 1713, one of those sons, Charles VI, promulgated the so-called Pragmatic Sanction to protect his daughter's inheritance. And in 1714, Louis XIV changed his will to legitimize his illegitimate offspring.

Ruling houses were also addicted to scouring their bloodlines and hunting for legal claims to upcoming successions, all employing learned genealogists and lawyers to assist them. In the case of Brunswick-Lüneburg-Calenberg, the family tree offered many promising connections: to the duchy of Lüneburg-Celle, to the Rhenish Palatinate and to the Kingdoms of Bohemia, Denmark and France. When George Augustus was old enough to understand, his grandmother Sophie would have told him that she, in addition to being a princess Palatine, was equally a granddaughter of James VI and I, and hence a claimant in the British Stuarts' line of succession. She may or may not have let on that she was preceded in the Stuart line by thirty or forty better-placed claimants. At

the time, the Stuart connection could hardly have been anything beyond a curiosity.

Importantly, however, all lines of succession are fluid, alter-
ing with every relevant birth, death and legal tweak. So the
Stuart Succession was not the same in 1683 as it later became.
When George Augustus was born, the ageing Charles II, King
of England, Scotland and Ireland, had no immediate heir; his
Catholic brother, James, Duke of York was childless; his Protestant nieces, Mary and Anne, were both newly-weds; and his
illegitimate son, James, Duke of Monmouth, was also har-
bouring a claim.[11]

The court in the Leineschloss was fully informed of developments. Duchess Sophie, raised in the Netherlands by exiled
parents, had remained – like her brother-in-law, Georg Wilhelm - a lifelong confidante of Mary's husband, William of
Orange.[12] What is more, her son, Georg Ludwig von Welf, had
been sent to England in 1680 as a potential bridegroom for
Princess Anne. But each family recoiled. Anne Stuart duly
married Prince George of Denmark, and Georg Ludwig, submitting to a family compact, married his cousin, the recently
legitimized Sophie Dorothea of Celle. The 'Hanoverian
Guelphs' had chosen a matrimonial strategy that put the con-
solidation of their local inheritance before riskier adventures
abroad. George Augustus's birth was the first fruit of that
strategy. His parents' marriage was variously described as 'disastrous', a 'mésalliance' and 'a complete failure'[13] and his life
began with no expectation of succeeding to a foreign title.

2
1683–1714: Thirty-one Rungs of the Ladder

As a prince in the making, George Augustus received more than the standard upbringing of average German noblemen.[1] Duke Ernst August and the Duchess Sophia held the reins. The child's parents were frequently absent. For four years, he developed under the care of Sophia's *Oberhofmeisterin*, before passing under the regime of private preceptors, including Philip von der Eltz, who taught his classes and slept protectively in a neighbouring room. He was sometimes joined by his younger sister and other noble-born children, dividing their time between the old Leineschloss and the summer palace of Herrenhausen, five miles away, which was being renovated.[2]

On Ernst August's orders, instruction in the Lutheran religion had priority. (By tradition, ruling Protestant princes held the position of *Summus Episcopus* or Chief Bishop of their principality's state Church.) Next came energetic sessions with the riding master, the fencing master and the dancing master. Academic studies began with reading and writing in French and the classics, followed by maths and modern languages – German, Italian and, at his grandmother's behest, English. Genealogy and heraldry were also emphasized. The court calendar provided a busy round of church services, religious festivals, hunting parties, baronial feasts, masques, carnivals, balls, concerts and parades. Aged sixteen, the adolescent started training as a cadet in one of the duke's elite cavalry units.

As manhood loomed, it became apparent that George Augustus did not enjoy his father's good looks. He was short and sturdy, ruddy-faced, endowed with thick legs, oversized hands and wide-set eyes that 'bulged like pigeon eggs', and worryingly bad tempered.[3] He therefore was no lady's dream, but he was fit and active, devoted to music, ceremony and hunting in the vast Göhrde Forest, where mouflon roamed, and eminently marriageable.

And role models abounded. Memories of the Thirty Years War were still alive, and people would talk of the 'Great Condé', victor of Rocroi, and of Turenne, Wallenstein and Gustavus Adolphus, the 'Lion of the North'. Duchess Sophia would tell her grandson of her late brother, Prince Rupert of the Rhine (1619–82), the dashing Royalist general of the English Civil War, admiral during the Restoration and Governor of distant Hudson's Bay.[4]

George Augustus was surrounded by kinsmen and neighbours, who all followed the warrior tradition. One uncle, Friedrich August (1661–90), was soon to be killed young, campaigning in Transylvania; another, Maximilian Wilhelm (1666–1726), was to command the Imperial cavalry at Blenheim. His neighbours at Wolfenbüttel produced an extraordinary number of prominent soldiers in the Imperial, Prussian, Dutch or Danish service, including Field Marshal Ferdinand Albert II (1680–1735); August Wilhelm, Duke of

Wolfenbüttel-Bevern (1715–81), a favourite of Frederick the
Great; and the brothers Ludwig Ernst (1718–88), known as
'Fat Louis', and Ferdinand (1721–92), both field marshals
and both known as the Duke of Brunswick. Above all,
George Augustus watched the careers of his nearest contemporaries: August der Starke, Duke-elector of Saxony
(1670–1733), Frederick William of Brandenburg-Prussia
(1688–1740), the future 'Soldier King', and Charles XII of
Sweden (1682–1718), his grandmother's relative, already
crowned before George Augustus joined his regiment.

As George Augustus grew up during the tumultuous
high noon of the Sun King's reign,[5] Europe was dislocated
by incessant war; the Empire reeled, and Brunswick-
Lüneburg was dangerously exposed. With uncertainties
multiplying, the Calenbergs hacked their way through a
dense undergrowth of domestic, military and international
events. Their principal concern revolved round the Holy
Roman Empire and their duchy's position within it. After
that, they closely followed the unpredictable twists and
turns of war and diplomacy, with particular regard to the
anti-French coalition, to which they belonged. And, like all
ambitious dynasties, they watched the royal and aristocratic marriage market like hawks, noting every birth,
death and matrimonial alliance that could affect Europe's
key lines of succession.

In the first decade of his life, George Augustus could
only have perceived his surroundings from the limited perspective of a child. He could have understood neither his
grandfather's dogged efforts to raise money and troops
and to win the emperor's favour nor the implications of

the Wars of Reunion, the Edict of Nantes or the League of Augsburg. But he would have quickly been impressed by the role of armies and the importance within society of status, hierarchy and precedence. He would have seen soldiers marching and drilling, and cavalrymen prancing, and have been stirred by the sound of fife and drum. He would have learned about the world beyond Hanover through the medium of French, hearing such names and terms as 'Christophe Colomb', 'Le Roi Soleil', 'Les Pays-Bas', and above all 'Le Saint-Empire'. It is impossible to say when he first heard of 'L'Angleterre', but it is very likely, aged five, that he would have been told how his grandmother's old friend, Guillaume-Willem, had sailed across the sea to be crowned king. Four years later, without grasping the details, he would certainly have been swept up in the wave of celebrations prompted by his grandfather's appointment as *Électeur présomptif*, or 'gewählter Kurfurst', an elector-elect.

1683 Spain declares war on France. The Ottomans overrun Hungary, and lay siege to Vienna. In England, discovery of the Rye House Plot to murder King Charles II.

1684 War of the Reunions ends, leaving Strasbourg in French hands. Netherlands devastated. Genoa bombarded. Pope founds the Holy League to fight the Ottomans.[6]

1685 Revoking the Edict of Nantes, Louis XIV enflames religious passions far beyond France. James II, a Roman Catholic, succeeds to the English throne. Georg Ludwig's cousin, Liselotte, marries Louis XIV's brother. George Augustus's parents tour Italy.

1686 Emperor Leopold retakes Buda and convenes the League of
Augsburg, forerunner of the Grand Alliance. Hamburg
besieged by the Danes.

1687 Turks routed at Mohács. Declaration of Indulgence in England introduces general toleration, disturbing Protestant
opinion. Birth of George Augustus's sister, Sophia Dorothea.

1688 France invades the Palatinate, Duchess Sophia's ancestral
home. The birth of James II's son frightens English Protestants, triggering William of Orange's expedition to England.

1689 England's 'Glorious Revolution' and Bill of Rights: William
and Mary co-monarchs.[7] Birth of Princess Anne's son. Louis
XIV declares war on England and Spain. Russia joins the
Empire against the Ottomans. Austria, the Dutch Republic
and Great Britain form the anti-French Grand Alliance.

1690 The emperor's son Joseph crowned King of the Romans. The
French disperse the Royal Navy off Beachy Head and defeat
the Savoyards in Piedmont. William of Orange triumphs at
the Battle of the Boyne. Ottomans regain Belgrade.

1691 Treaty of Limerick pacifies the British Isles. French forces
make gains from the Dutch and from Savoy and launch
raids across the Rhine.

1692 Royal Navy thwarts Louis XIV's invasion plans. Massacre
of Glencoe. Stadtholder-king William loses Namur. Duke
Ernst August of Calenberg designated the ninth Imperial
elector. George Augustus becomes heir apparent to the electoral heir apparent.[8]

The elevation of the Calenberg Guelphs to electoral rank in
1692 undoubtedly marked a significant milestone. Poten-
tially, it gave them equal standing with the Empire's four

other secular electors – the Palatines, Brandenburgers, Saxons and Bavarians – and raised them above their smarting Wolfenbüttel neighbours. Yet they had to await confirmation by the Imperial Diet, and their advancement, which was legally contested, implied increased military contributions. In Wolfenbüttel, Ernst August would still have been regarded as the Fürst von Calenberg, not yet as Kurfürst.

Meanwhile, speculation surrounding the English Succession abated. William of Orange had rebuffed the Jacobites; his sister-in-law Anne was still bearing children, and her son, William of Gloucester, was healthy. The Stuarts had been effectively deposed. The Calenbergs had no special reason to pay attention to English affairs, though the international scene remained fluid.

1693 The Grand Alliance falters. William of Orange repulsed at Neerwinden. Anglo-Dutch naval convoy ambushed off Gibraltar. Eugene of Savoy appointed Imperial field marshal.

1694 The continental War of the Grand Alliance stagnates. In England, Queen Mary's death leaves William as sole sovereign.[9] In Hanover, the Königsmarck Affair leads to the incarceration of George Augustus's mother, Sophia Dorothea of Celle, and to the foul murder of her lover, Count Königsmarck. George Augustus never sees his mother again.[10]

1695 William of Orange brilliantly recaptures the Vauban-designed fortress of Namur, his greatest military achievement. The wars move towards stalemate.

1696 France makes peace with Savoy; William of Orange accepts Swedish mediation. The King of Poland dies, prompting a royal election; the Calenbergs' neighbour, the Duke-elector of Saxony, declares his candidacy with Russian support.

1697 France and the Grand Alliance sign the Treaty of Ryswick, initiating peace. Prince Eugene annihilates the Ottomans at Zenta. The Saxon duke-elector wins the Polish election, converting to Catholicism and creating Europe's largest composite state in Saxony-Poland-Lithuania.[11] Charles XII accedes to the Swedish throne.

1698 In Spain, a childless king bequeaths his realms to Bavaria, while France conspires to partition his empire. In England, Queen Anne's miscarriages throw doubt on the Stuart Succession. William of Orange visits Brunswick-Lüneburg, hatching a provisional deal with the Electress Sophia. George Augustus meets the royal visitor. Duke Ernst August dies, making Georg Ludwig prince-elector and George Augustus electoral heir apparent.

During his early teenage years, therefore, George Augustus would not have been burdened unduly by thoughts of the future, other than by his prospective role as his father's son and soldier prince. Yet he can hardly have been indifferent to his meeting, aged fifteen, with William of Orange, however brief. For 'Oncle Guillaume', as he would perhaps have known him, was now presented as *Sa Majesté le Roi* and would have been surrounded by much whispering and deference. Three years later, aged eighteen, the boy would certainly have been privy to the implications for his family of England's *Acte d'Établissement*, though it is interesting to wonder in what terms the dowager duchess's new dignity would have been defined. In all probability, George Augustus would first have heard of his grandmother being described as 'l'Héritière désignée du trône anglais' and of himself as 'Héritier de l'Héritier de la Héritière'.

1699 The Bavarian elector dies, provoking more treaties of Spanish partition. Russia, Denmark and Poland agree to partition the Swedish Empire. In Hanover, the Calenbergs' Catholic niece, Wilhelmina Amalia, marries the emperor's heir, Archduke Joseph. Peace of Karlowitz in the East; renewed war looming in the West.

1700 Both the War of the Spanish Succession[12] and the Great Northern War[13] erupt. The deaths of Spain's King Charles the Bedevilled and England's royal heir, Prince William, start new dynastic crises. The Hohenzollerns demand royal status. William of Orange summons Duchess Sophia to Apeldoorn to outline his 'Hanoverian Project'.

1701 The Grand Alliance is renewed. Louis XIV's grandson, Philip V, enters Madrid. James Edward Stuart, the 'Old Pretender', recognized in France as King of England. French forces seize the 'barrier fortresses' on the Dutch frontier. Peter I founds St Petersburg on Swedish soil. Guided by the stadtholder-king, the English Parliament promulgates the Act of Settlement, disinheriting dozens of Catholic Stuarts and naming, as Princess Anne's successor, George Augustus's seventy-one-year-old grandmother: 'the most excellent Princess Sophia, Electress and Dowager Duchess of Hanover, ... [granddaughter] of our late sovereign lord King James I of happy memory ... and the heirs of her body, being Protestants'.[14]

Thus, in the eighteenth century's second year, the Calenbergs moved up a further notch in the international rankings. They were electors-designate but not yet electors: heirs presumptive to the English and Irish kingdoms, though not of Scotland, and not yet kings. They were hedging their bets between Wilhelmina Amalia's Catholic Habsburg connection and the Protestant English connection. Further progress was entirely dependent on the life expectancy of several individuals and on the fickle fortunes of war. Should William of Orange be defeated, the exiled Stuarts would retake England under French protection and the 'Hanoverian Project' would be scrapped.

The choice of the Dowager Duchess Sophia by the English Parliament was determined as much by political as by purely genealogical considerations: her late husband, Duke-elector Ernst August and his brother, Georg Wilhelm, had been William III's staunch allies during the recent Nine Years War. She also held the important advantage of possessing two generations of healthy male heirs. Beyond that, from the perspective of the 'Hanoverian Project', many other features of her family tree were best forgotten. As her parents' thirteenth child, she was preceded in terms of inheritance by several older living siblings and/or their offspring. One of them, Louise Hollandine (1622–1709) was an unconventional Catholic painter-abbess living in France. Her late eldest brother, Charles-Louis, Elector Palatine (1617–80), had been a strong Cromwellian supporter during the English Civil War and had produced another brood of thirteen children. Her niece Liselotte, Duchess of Orleans (1652–1722) was married to Louis XIV's brother, and her Stuart grand-niece, Anne-Marie, Duchess of Savoy (1669–1728) was mother-in-law to Louis, le Petit Dauphin, Fils de France and soon-to-be father of the future Louis XV.

Nonetheless, amid skilful image-building, preparations went ahead: 'The Earl of Macclesfield was deputed by the King to carry the joyful intelligence, and the Order of the Garter for the Elector, to the court of Herenhausen, where he was received with the highest marks of distinction and rewarded with very rich and splendid presents.'[15]

The interests of the two parties were nicely convergent. The English Parliament was anxious to sponsor what it took to be malleable, Protestant monarchs. The Calenbergs, like other German princes, were dreaming of a powerful composite state. George Augustus saw the battles and political manoeuvres swirling around him, with no influence on their outcome. For, when the Act of Settlement was adopted, all remained to be accomplished. Another dozen years would pass in uncertainty.

1702 A Franco-Spanish fleet is destroyed by the Royal Navy at Vigo Bay. In Poland, the Swedes temporarily depose the Saxon king-elector. In London, the stadtholder-king's horse steps on a molehill, falls and kills its rider; Jacobites toast 'the little gentleman in velvet'. Queen Anne confirms Duchess Sophie as her heiress apparent.

1703 The Scottish parliament passes a Bill of Security blocking England's Act of Settlement. In November the 'Great Storm' kills 8,000 English people; Queen Anne awakened in St James's Palace as the roof blows off.

1704 Anglo-Dutch troops capture the Spanish fortress of Gibraltar. Vienna threatened by a Hungarian revolt. A Franco-Bavarian campaign is halted by the spectacular Allied victory at Blenheim.[17] John Churchill, the victor of Blenheim, created Duke of Marlborough.[18]

1705 Emperor Leopold I succeeded by Joseph I, husband of the Calenbergs' relative, Wilhelmina Amalia. Commissioners discuss a constitutional union between England and Scotland. In June, George Augustus travels incognito to Ansbach to observe the twenty-two-year-old Princess Caroline. The young couple defy family pressures and are married in Hanover in September. Following the death of Duke Georg Wilhelm, the duchy of Celle is merged with Calenberg, significantly enlarging the prospective Electorate.

1706 The Grand Alliance's *annus mirabilis*. France sues for peace. At Ramillies in May Marlborough's Anglo-Dutch-Danish army triumphs. In England, following the Sophia Naturalisation Act, Parliament urges the heiress to reside in London, but Queen Anne objects. George Augustus is handed several English titles, including Duke of Cambridge.[19]

1707 The Act of Union joins England with Scotland to form the Kingdom of Great Britain.[20] Provisions made for a Regency Council. In Vienna, syphilis renders the Imperial couple sterile. George Augustus's wife Caroline, in contrast, gives birth to their son, Frederick. He himself, his dynastic duty performed, is freed for military service.

1708 Marlborough and Prince Eugene join forces in July to defeat the French at Oudenarde. George Augustus distinguishes himself in the battle at the head of the ducal cavalry.[21] Shortly afterwards, in the *Reichssaal* at Regensburg, the Imperial Diet finally confirms the electoral status of the Calenbergs' duchy.

In the third decade of his life, therefore, George Augustus, already adult and married, went to war and fathered a family, watching from afar as the English connection promised much but delivered little. Implementation of the Hanoverian Project remained elusive for years. Its main sponsors, the English Whigs, met opposition from the queen, the Tories and the Scots. Desperately wanting a Hanoverian presence in Britain, they repeatedly invited George Augustus to London, but were never allowed to receive him. The fortunes of war long remained indecisive. In 1708 at Oudenarde, fighting under Marlborough's command, the young prince earned himself a name and some lines from Jonathan Swift:

> Not so did behave
> Young Hanover brave
> In this bloody Field,
> I assure ye
> When his War-horse was shot
> He valued it not
> But fought still on foot
> Like a fury.[16]

But France did not make a truce with England until 1712, nor peace with the Empire until two years later.

1709 Marlborough and Eugene triumph at Malplaquet. At Poltava, the unrated Russian army annihilates the Swedes. The Russians restore the Saxon king-elector to his Polish throne.

1710 George Augustus's father announces his intention of inheriting the British throne by hereditary right, not by will of

Parliament. An Allied expeditionary force puts Archduke Charles on to the Spanish throne.

1711   Amid universal exhaustion, a smallpox epidemic claims many victims including Emperor Joseph I and Louis XIV's heir, Louis, le Grand Dauphin. Under Emperor Charles, the Calenbergs' influence in Vienna dwindles. In London the Tories rally, Marlborough is dismissed and Robert Walpole imprisoned.

1712   Peace negotiations open at Utrecht. Close to Brunswick-Lüneburg, Danish troops seize the Swedish possessions of Bremen and Verden, which are put up for sale.[22]

1713   The Peace of Utrecht is arranged through a series of bilateral treaties: Philip V is recognized as King of Spain; Austria takes the Spanish Netherlands, Milan and Naples; Britain, Gibraltar and Minorca; and Savoy, Sicily.[23] The emperor reissues the Pragmatic Sanction. Frederick William I is confirmed as Prussian king. Swedes defeated by the Danes at Oldenburg; Russian and Saxon troops capture Swedish Stettin.

1714   In Britain, the fall of Queen Anne's Tory administration weakens opposition to the Hanoverian Succession. The Peace of Utrecht finalized by the Treaty of Baden (September).

During the long years of the War of the Spanish Succession, George Augustus's first brush with Britain cannot have pleased him one bit. He penned a Latin note thanking Queen Anne for her gift of the Garter, which came with the title of Duke of Cambridge, and was no doubt flattered to see the Duke of Marlborough among his would-be hosts. Yet the crude attempts at manipulation can only have appalled him. His father's envoy in London, Baron Schütz, was to tell the House of Lords (falsely) that 'the young Prince is already on his way to reside in these realms' and was duly expelled.[24] The prince-duke made no public comment, but one imagines him thinking: 'Just you wait! The time may come when I will make the decisions.'

As diplomacy was rebooted, hostilities in Europe wound down. Louis XIV's hegemonial dreams perished; the Habsburgs pruned their ambitions, and Great Britain and the Netherlands finally felt secure. Having lost out in the Empire, the Calenbergs held their breath over the chances of a Hanoverian Succession in Great Britain. Queen Anne could neither produce a new heir nor bear to support the elderly dowager duchess wholeheartedly. The duchess would have known an old proverb, 'Il y a loin de la coupe aux lèvres' – 'There's many a slip 'twixt cup and lip.'

Early in 1714, British politics was in uproar. Queen Anne had lost patience with the Tories, without regaining confidence in the rival Whig Party, which had supported both the Grand Alliance and the 'Hanoverian Project'. A clause in the Treaty of Utrecht upheld the Hanoverian Succession, but Queen Anne still forbade the Calenbergs to visit her.[25]

Matters came to a head in the summer. The Dowager Duchess Sophia, who had once dreamed of the words 'Queen of England' adorning her coffin, now complained of receiving 'nothing but sheets of parchment', and in late May was further upset by a personal letter from Queen Anne:

Madam, Sister, Aunt, Since the right of succession to my kingdom has been fixed on you ... there have always been disaffected persons, who [want] to have a prince of your blood in my dominions ... I should tell you that such a proceeding will infallibly draw along consequences dangerous to that succession itself, which is not secure [unless] the prince who ... wears the crown maintains her authority and prerogative.[26]

The message reeked with mistrust. Reports arrived that the queen 'preferred the Pretender to the Hanover', and that the Stuarts could still snatch the prize by a timely religious conversion. The duchess would have appreciated the irony that the 'Hanoverian Project' was kept afloat by the Pretender's Jesuit confessors. Thereupon, having caught cold in the Herrenhausen gardens, she passed away aged eighty-three on 8 June. Her son became the British heir apparent on the spot: 'The death of the electress taking place at this period, the elector of Brunswic was, by order of the Court, prayed for by name in all churches and chapels throughout England.'[27]

Georg Ludwig exercised his rights under the Crown Succession Act by naming seven extra 'Lords Justice' to join the Regency Council. The act, passed seven years earlier, made it treason to deny or to oppose the Act of Settlement.

Then suddenly, on 1 August, Queen Anne herself expired. Georg Ludwig succeeded automatically, and his thirty-year-old son became heir apparent both to the Electorate and the kingdoms. The Calenberg Guelphs stood at the threshold of a new Personal Union and Dual Authority. Europe's latest composite state was coming into the world. And its ruling family, sold to the English and the British as the 'Hanoverians', was bound for a new international career.

For George Augustus, however, the prospects were daunting. He had never visited England; the only Britishers he had ever met were the officers of Marlborough's army, the occasional emissaries sent to Herrenhausen, and his own English mistress, Henrietta Howard (1689–1767). Equally, for the British public, the 'Hanoverian prince' was almost unknown, except for his exploits at Oudenarde. Britishers were not well attuned to the intricacies of continental politics, which most concerned him, nor to life in a principality constantly threatened with foreign occupation. Though his engraved portrait circulated, nobody knew the first thing either about his touchy temperament or about the subterraneal secrets of his dysfunctional family.

3
1714–1727: Apprenticeship

The transposition of royalty from country to country was a commonplace event in early modern Europe. It was the experience of every English or British queen from Anne of Denmark in 1589 to Adelaide of Saxe-Meiningen in 1818. Almost as frequent were the removals of monarchs' households. In 1603, James VI and I transported his vast entourage from Edinburgh to London. In May 1660, King Charles II brought over his court from Holland, as did William of Orange in 1688. So the removal of the king-elector's court from Hanover to London in 1714 was not specially remarkable.

Multiple unions of crowns were commonplace, too. In the British Isles, with one interval, the Stuarts had ruled from 1603 to 1707 over a triple union. William of Orange introduced a quadruple union. Queen Anne reverted in 1707 to the dual union of Great Britain and Ireland. So the reappearance in 1714 of a tripartite political contraption uniting Great Britain, Ireland and Brunswick-Lüneburg should not have been too difficult to comprehend.

The prince-elector, Georg Ludwig, now styled 'King George I', arrived in England on 18 September 1714 (Old

Style),* in the eighteenth year of his ducal lordship and on the forty-ninth day of his royal reign.[1] His household, including George Augustus, landed at Greenwich, arousing much interest. Conspicuously, the king-elector, a tall, handsome man, had no queen-electress by his side. Instead, two ladies appeared, one thin and one fat, instantly dubbed 'the May-pole' and 'the Elephant', and both mistaken for mistresses. Actually, the trim Sophia von Kielmansegg was his half-sister, the portly Melusine von der Schulenberg the *maîtresse-en-titre*. A dwarf jester and two turbaned Turkish valets accompanied fifteen high Hanoverian officials, charged with running the Electorate from afar.

A parliamentary delegation fell deferentially to their knees. Noting the incident, a Victorian historian commented on 'the strange religion of king-worship' once prevalent.[2] George Augustus saw for himself how strong the monarchical element still was within the constitutional order.

Addressing the Privy Council, the king-elector pointedly ignored the Act of Settlement, stating baldly that he possessed his 'ancestral lands' by right. Making common cause with the Whig Party, he skilfully exploited their inability to put their theories of parliamentary supremacy before the 'Hanoverian Project'. Queen Anne's Stuart-leaning Tory

---

* Up to 1751, England clung to the Old Style Julian Calendar, which was eleven days behind the New Style Gregorian Calendar that was current in most other European countries, including Scotland.

ministers fell into disfavour. Robert Harley would be impeached; Bolingbroke fled abroad.

The coronation in Westminster Abbey on 20 October 1714 was marked by a medal showing Britannia crowning the monarch. George Augustus, wearing Queen Mary's crown for the occasion, and Caroline – now Prince and Princess of Wales – joined the peerage. Widespread protests and a torrent of anti-Hanoverian pamphlets prompted the infamous Riot Act.[3]

George Augustus, aged thirty-one, was allocated quarters alongside his father in St James's Palace. Caroline soon arrived with their three little daughters: Anne aged five, Amelia, three, and Caroline, one. Their living conditions were less spacious than in Calenberg Castle, and psychologically cramped by the presence of Henrietta Howard, once a refugee in Hanover from domestic abuse, who now served both the prince as mistress and the princess as lady-in-waiting.[4] The couple suffered greater distress from the absence of their seven-year-old son, Friedrich (Frederick), whom the king-elector had ordered to stay in Hanover, against his parents' wishes. The family's proximity to the monarch only increased their unease. George Augustus, eternally offended by his father's high-handedness, and particularly by his mother's continuing incarceration, never enjoyed a comfortable filial relationship. By 1714, his mother, Sophia Dorothea, had already been imprisoned for twenty years, closely guarded in Schloss Ahlden and forbidden to communicate with her two children. George Augustus's genuine pain derived not merely from his mother's hopeless predicament but equally from his father's incurably vengeful attitude. As reported, 'The Prince's greatest crime in the eyes of his father was the respect and affection which he invariably showed for his unfortunate mother, Sophia of Zell.'[5]

Nonetheless, the heir apparent's household took well to their unfamiliar surroundings. They developed an interest in British affairs, welcomed local people as advisers, and improved their language skills. Unlike his father, cruelly lampooned as 'Cuckoldy George' on account of the Königsmarck Affair, the prince displayed a conventional family life and spoke passable English, though with an accent variously described as 'bluff Westphalian' and 'execrable'. While proclaiming himself to be purely English,[6] he spoke French within the family, German to his Hanoverian officials, and dog Latin where necessary. From the start, the ambiance was multilingual.

In the winter of 1714–15, political storm clouds gathered. The belief grew that the Stuarts had been cheated; a general election gave the Whigs a strong majority, exasperating the Jacobites; and Scottish resentments overflowed. The Earl of Mar raised the standard of 'King James VIII' at Braemar in September. His army of Gaelic clansmen and Jacobites overran the Highlands, survived the clash with Hanoverian loyalists at Sheriffmuir, invaded northern England and eventually surrendered in Lancashire.[7]

The government's mild response to the 'Fifteen' was well judged. Few rebels were executed, though many suffered forfeiture or transportation to the West Indies. An Act of Indemnity (1717) cleared the air, and a silver medal proclaimed CLEMENTIA AUGUSTI. Remote Glen Shiel witnessed the last whimper of resistance. And the 'Hanoverians' gained a generation of calm.

A botched attempt to kill George Augustus further assisted the Hanoverian cause. On 8 December 1716, a man called Freeman entered the prince's box at Drury Lane Theatre, discharging a shot that flew past his head. The press declared Freeman 'mad' and praised the prince's coolness under fire.[8] The incident occurred at a delicate juncture. In the rebellion's aftermath, Anglican pulpits were breathing fire against Papists and Jacobites; Roman Catholics were being forced to register their property and take oaths of allegiance, and the Forfeited Estates Commission was hard at work.[9] Freeman's miss proved symbolic. The rebellion, too, had misfired.

For a time, the royal and electoral family could relax. In 1716–17, during the monarch's first absence in Germany, George Augustus was appointed 'Guardian and Lieutenant of the Realm' with limited powers, and embarked on an official progress round southern England. He saw how the kingdom lived from international commerce and finance, familiarizing himself with the Bank of England, the Royal Exchange and the National Debt. At Woolwich dockyard he clambered aboard the ninety-gun, triple-decked ship of the line HMS *Prince George*, renamed in his honour, glimpsing the Royal Navy's massive capacities. In matters of governance, he would have seen that Parliament alone could not bypass the royal prerogatives, and that British law was irrelevant in the Electorate. He observed how his father's court remained the focus of political and upper-class social life. He dropped the late Queen Anne's custom of holding séances to bestow the 'Royal Touch',[10] but, in the style of Louis XIV, let in the crowds to gape as he dined.[11]

George Augustus cannot have failed to spot a tendency among the locals to inflate the importance of their country and to denigrate his own. Even today, English historians can say that he came from 'a dinky little German principality',[12] or assume that Britain was already a superpower.

The only regular job which George Augustus held from 1715 to 1718 was that of Governor of the South Sea Company, whose shares were fast becoming the object of immoderate speculation. He resigned in favour of his father before the 'South Sea Bubble' burst two years later, but not before making contact with Sir Robert Walpole, a prominent investor. He then chaired an ineffective board of inquiry into ministerial financial abuse, on to which he co-opted Walpole. Yet his overall frustration was growing. His advice was no longer being sought; he felt sidelined by his father's ministers.

In 1717, therefore, George Augustus lost patience and became embroiled in a protracted feud with his father, which started through a trivial argument over the choice of godparents for the prince's newborn son. The prince and princess stormed out of the christening ceremony. In retaliation, the king-elector banned them from his palace and kidnapped their three young children.[13] The balladeers broke into song:

> God prosper long our noble King,
> His Turks and Germans all.
> A woeful christ'ning late there did
> In James's house befall . . .[14]

Contemporary monarchs often behaved outrageously. George Augustus's youthful nephew, Frederick of Prussia, was forced by a cruel father to witness his best friend's beheading.

The Prince and Princess of Wales thereon set up an alternative court at their new residence, Leicester House, watching it develop as the focus for both cultural activities and dissident politics.[15] Princess Caroline, a forceful and intelligent personality destined to be Britain's 'funniest, cleverest and fattest queen', who once adjudicated in a disputation between Isaac Newton and Gottfried Leibniz, would now star as London's glittering social hostess. In the 1720s she gave birth to three more children, benefiting from a handsome personal allowance of £100,000 per annum arranged by Robert Walpole.[16] (Today's equivalent would be over £12 million.)

By 1720, Walpole was establishing himself as the chief political fixer in the land, securing lucrative Treasury posts and consolidating the Whig Party's alliance with the ruling family. By the timely sale of his South Sea shares, he had amassed a colossal fortune enabling him to reconstruct his palatial residence at Holkham Hall in Norfolk, and to start a superb art collection, which, later sold to Russia, would form the core of the Hermitage holdings.[17]

Walpole, in fact, was the only person who could rise above the rivalry of the two royal courts and engineer a reconciliation. Firstly, he extracted the vast sum of £600,000 from Parliament for eliminating royal debts; secondly, in late 1720, just before the South Sea Bubble burst, he organized a personal meeting in the king-elector's private chamber. The prince said (in French): 'It has been a very great grief to be in His Majesty's displeasure.' The king-elector mumbled something about '*Votre conduite*' ('Your behaviour'), using the formal second person plural. The prince was left guessing whether or not forgiveness had happened. But an apology was recorded, and the money paid over. Caroline told her ladies that her husband had been bribed. The king-elector started to re-embellish Kensington Palace with the help of the 'pushy painter', William Kent. He then ruled that no one could attend both his own court and that of his son. George Augustus headed the proscribed list. So the split did not really heal.

By 1721, Walpole was reaching what one of his successors would call 'the top of the greasy pole'. Unequalled as a parliamentarian and unscathed by the South Sea Company's collapse, he dominated the government, appointed by the king-elector as First Lord of the Treasury, with his brother-in-law Townsend as Northern Secretary. Furthermore, since the monarch frequently missed Cabinet meetings, Walpole started to assume the chair. This set-up, known to contemporaries as the 'Robinocracy',[18] gradually associated him with the new title of 'Prime Minister'.[19] For George Augustus, Walpole, 'whom nothing terrified and nothing astonished' and who was epitomized by his motto of *Quieta non movere*, was a worthy teacher in the political arts.[20]

Meanwhile, Princess Caroline came into her own as the centrepiece of London's most lively artistic salon – full of mirth, repartee and intellectual curiosity, and by now speaking English 'uncommonly well'. Of the princely pair, she was the celebrity, George Augustus the dapper and sometimes peevish addendum. Their house resembled 'a university seminar';

her guests included Newton, Pope, Montesquieu and Handel. She cultivated Walpole, while the prince depended on Spencer Compton, the Commons' Speaker and future Earl of Wilmington. Their three Hanover-born daughters, still living with their grandfather, were joined by three further siblings – William, Duke of Cumberland (born 1721), Mary and Louise, whose elder brother, Frederick, could not visit London, nor his parents visit him.

George Augustus and Caroline were much preoccupied in the late 1720s by plans for Frederick's marriage, drawn up in Berlin by his aunt, the Prussian queen. Frederick (born 1708) was lined up with his cousin, Princess Friederike Wilhelmine (born in 1709), while the Prussian crown prince, the other Frederick (born in 1712), was to be matched with Princess Amelia (born in 1711). Yet, in correspondence, the 'King in Prussia' objected to Amelia being the second- and not the firstborn daughter. And in any case the scheme had little chance of realization during the lifetime of George Augustus's father.[21]

The king-elector rarely intervened in domestic politics, but keenly exercised his prerogative over foreign policy. Many European monarchs were his relations. The French regent from 1715 to 1723, Philippe d'Orléans, was cousin Liselotte's son. The Austrian empress was another distant cousin, the former Princess of Brunswick-Wolfenbüttel. And the queen in Prussia was his own daughter.

The senior Calenberg Guelph had reached Britain at the tail end of a generation of international conflict. Yet Louis XIV was now dead. His successor was a child, and French policy fell to Cardinal Fleury, 'le Pacifique'. Russia terminated the Northern Wars in 1721. Prussia was guarding its war chest. And an heirless emperor was preoccupied with securing his daughter's succession.

The leading members of the house of Brunswick-Lüneburg, therefore, could pause to take stock. They had eagerly accepted the British connection for reasons of dynastic aggrandizement, but also, geopolitically, to out-flank their homeland's traditional French enemy. They then found that France had lost its expansive appetite, and in 1716, to uphold the Treaty of Utrecht, saw fit to form an Anglo-French alliance, subsequently expanded. Spain alone proved difficult, precipitating a desultory Spanish War in 1718, which sent the Royal Navy into Mediterranean action.

Tensions with Spain persisted throughout the decade. Spanish patriots could not stomach the loss of Gibraltar. From the king-elector's perspective, the major issue for the kingdoms concerned Spain's failure to enforce the *Asiento de negros*, Britain's contract on the Atlantic slave trade. For the Electorate, the emperor's reluctance to finalize the trans-fer of Bremen and Verden was galling.[22] Then, in 1726, a second Anglo-Spanish War broke out. A Royal Navy squad-ron sailed to blockade Portobello in Panama. Spain laid the thirteenth siege of Gibraltar. Both actions would prove disastrous.

George Augustus was excluded from policymaking. But Walpole's wisdom was self-evident. Ruinous large-scale conflicts were to be avoided. The Electorate was safe so long as the French were quiescent. Naval strength kept the British Isles safe. Satisfaction was in order.[23]

On 25 March 1727 George Augustus and Caroline celebrated New Year's Day Old Style – a natural moment for reflection. They would recently have heard with no small bitterness of the death of George Augustus's mother, Sophia Dorothea, with whom they had never been allowed to communicate. Assessing their own progress, they would undoubtedly have compared themselves above all to their German neighbours. Their detested brother-in-law in Berlin, Frederick William, the 'Soldier King', was not soldiering; they disapproved both of his brutality towards his children and of his objections to the Prusso-Hanoverian marriage scheme, sympathizing with the Prussian queen, George Augustus's sister, who by now had borne fourteen children. Their neighbour in Denmark-Oldenburg, Frederick IV (r. 1699–1730), was mired in Swedish wars and complex romances. Another neighbour, Augustus II of Saxony-Poland-Lithuania, had submitted to Russian control. Nine years previously, Charles XII of Sweden had perished on the snowy battlements of a Norwegian fortress, killed by a sniper's bullet.[24] His death gave the Swedish throne to still more neighbours, the Hesse-Kassels.[25]

By the standards of the day, George Augustus's father, at sixty-seven, was growing old, and the heir apparent must surely have been eyeing the future. Yet his hopes and fears would have centred on the prospects for preserving the whole of his dynastic inheritance, not just on 'Merry England'. Almost certainly, he suspected his father of hostile intentions, and knew full well that some of his British subjects still dreamed of alternatives. But he, not they, would be in charge.

This was a time, if not earlier, when George Augustus and Caroline could have perused the latest edition of Chamberlayne's *Magnae Britanniae Notitia* – an annually published constitutional compendium, a sort of early Bagehot, and a handbook for future monarchs. Under 'Power and Prerogative', they could have read:

> The King alone by his Royal Prerogative hath power, without Act of Parliament, to declare war, make peace, send and receive Ambassadors ... to make Leagues and Treaties ... [to] levy Men and Arms ... [to] convoke, prorogue, and dissolve Parliaments ... [to nominate] all Commanders, Magistrates, Counsellors, Officers of State ... [and] Bishops ... [to bestow] all honours, and punishments ... [to convene] Synods ... [and to] correct all heresies ...[26]

By way of limitations, they could see:

> Every King of England, as he is *Debiter Justiciae* to his People, so he is in conscience obliged to defend and maintain all Rights of the Crown in Possession; and when any King hath not religiously observed his Duty ... it hath proved of dreadful consequence. [On the other hand], it much concerns every King ... to [observe] the Golden Rule of Charles I, that 'the King's Prerogative is to defend the People's Liberties, and the People's Liberties to strengthen the King's Prerogatives' ... Two things especially the King ... cannot do without the Consent of both Houses of Parliament, viz make new Laws and raise new Taxes, there being something of Odium in both of them ...[27]

One imagines Caroline questioning Chamberlayne's authority to write so indicatively, and George Augustus commenting laconically, 'Pas si mal.'

Throughout the spring of 1727, special government messengers brought the king-elector regular updates on the Spanish war. At Gibraltar, the Spanish bombardiers were making no headway. So in early June, unworried, he left London for Hanover as planned.

Ten days later, George Augustus and Caroline were taking an afternoon nap in their summer retreat at Richmond Lodge. The sound of galloping hooves filled the park, before a breathless Robert Walpole dismounted, stamped the dust from his riding boots and demanded an audience. Bowing low, he broke the news from Osnabrück that the prince's father was dead. Rightly or wrongly, the new king-elector was reported as saying, grumpily: '*Dat* is a lie!'

George Augustus's apprenticeship in the royal trade had given him little hands-on experience and failed to cure the family rifts. His unforgiving father had departed without a word of encouragement; his disgruntled son Frederick would soon arrive to turn up the stress. Although George Augustus had not been seen in Germany for the last thirteen years, the British public had learned more about him. They knew him to be outwardly presentable, to love the theatre and military parades, and to be liable to tantrums. Stories were going around about him furiously kicking his hat around or stamping on his wig; he was so accustomed to bottling up his private thoughts that he was always liable to periodic, unstatesmanlike eruptions. As to his inner life, everyone, including his modern biographers, could only speculate. Any intelligent observer knows that the victims of childhood trauma, long hidden, run the risk of maltreating their own offspring in intergenerational abuse. In quieter moments, he might even have thought about it himself.

4
1727–1760: On the Throne, Part I – Courtiers, Clerics, Sixpence and Slaves

OVERTURE

The reign of George II Augustus began with two proclamations. In Hanover, even before the old monarch's funeral, electoral officials staged the proclamation of his successor, made from the balcony of the Leineschloss; it added *König Georg der Zweiter von Gross-britannien und Irland* to his ducal and Imperial titles, and was followed by a ceremony of homage. In London, the traditional proclamation was read out on the morning of 14 June 1727 Old Style in the courtyard of Leicester House:

> Whereas it has pleased Almighty God to call to his Mercy our late Sovereign Lord, King George of Blessed Memory . . . We, therefore . . . with one full voice and consent of Heart and Tongue, do Publish and Proclaim, That the High and Mighty George, Prince of Wales . . . is now become Our only lawful and rightful Liege Lord, George the Second, King of Great Britain, France and Ireland, Defender of the Faith etc . . .[1]

The same words were read out throughout the land, including at St Helier in Jersey, on the exact spot where the monarch's gilded statue now stands.[2]

The Privy Council of Great Britain then assembled to hear the king-elector's speech and the councillors' Oath of Allegiance, which bound them both to personal loyalty and to the disclosure of others' disloyalty. Whereupon the Archbishop of Canterbury, William Wake, stepped forward to hand over the late monarch's last will and testament, expecting the king-elector to read out the contents. Instead, George Augustus thanked the archbishop politely, pocketed the document and spirited it away. He must surely have had wind of something untoward, probably from Vienna. Some British historians believe, dubiously, that anything in the will contrary to the Act of Settlement could have been invalidated. In the event, the will's contents were never disclosed and George Augustus never explained his action. Futile legal claims would long be pursued by the Prussian Queen, by Petronilla Schulenberg, Countess of Walsingham, Georg Ludwig's natural daughter, and by the widow of his Turkish valet.

The king-elector's coronation took place in Westminster Abbey on the morning of 11 (Old Style) 22 (New Style) October 1727. Portraits of the royal and electoral pair were painted by Charles Jervas. The procession, taking two hours to pass, was described by the Swiss visitor César de Saussure. The queen-electress, dripping with pearls and borrowed diamonds, was dressed by Henrietta Howard. The king-elector walked, like his wife, under a canopy of cloth of gold: 'The [king-elector wore] robes of purple velvet, lined and bordered with ermine. On his head was a cap of crimson velvet with a gold circlet . . . [which] was too large, and kept falling over his eyes. His Majesty was supported by the Bishops of Durham and St Asaph in cloaks, rochets and copes of silver cloth.'[3]

Acclamation, anointment, investment, crowning, homage and holy communion followed. The king's champion, Lewis Dymoke, mounted and clad in full armour, challenged all traitors to mortal combat.[4] And Georg Friedrich Handel (1685–1759), the family's *Kapellmeister*, composed four coronation anthems; one of them, 'Zadok the Priest', became a fixture at all future British coronations:

> Zadok the Priest, and Nathan the Prophet anointed Solomon King.
> And all the people rejoic'd, and said:
> God Save the King! Long live the King!
> May the King live for ever,
> Amen, Alleluia.[5]

Parallel festivities were again held in Hanover. Notables assembled in the Queen of Denmark's Apartments of the Leineschloss. Forgettable *Tafelmusik* by Venturini was played. Crowds in the *Holzmarkt* were greeted by Prince Frederick, standing in for his father. Alms were distributed, bells rung. Gun salutes roared out. Oxen, ducks and geese were roasted in the street. And the good burghers chose between red wine dispensed from the stony mouth of a royal lion and white wine pouring from the muzzle of an electoral horse.[6]

These scenes demonstrate that George Augustus was not

just a monarch of German origin living and reigning in London. From 1727, he reigned in Brunswick-Lüneburg as well as in Great Britain and Ireland, and always considered his Electorate to be an integral part of his life, his realms and his mental world. For the biographer, this means that it is not sufficient to present the king-elector's German background in the opening chapters on childhood and upbringing. It calls for the German aspects of every relevant theme to be expounded alongside the British ones from start to finish.

Biographers must also realize, since George Augustus left no diaries or memoirs, and rarely elaborated on his opinions, that a great deal has to be deduced from circumstance and from second-hand reports; indeed, they are obliged to resist the temptation to describe the events of the reign without trying to recreate the monarch's own perspective. In this regard, they have no alternative to summarizing the people and events with whom and which their subject interacted, as a necessary prelude to the reconstruction of his experiences, opinions, outlook and personality.

Heraldry reflected the new king-elector's status. The flags or standards of his principal realms were the Union Jack of Great Britain, the Golden Harp of Ireland and the White Horse of Brunswick. The royal arms of the Hanoverian Guelphs displayed an adjusted fourth quarter carrying the symbols of Brunswick, Lüneburg and Westphalia, and the crown of the Holy Roman Empire.[7] A Hanoverian horse was inserted into a central panel on the ensigns of the British armed services. The pedantic heart of George Augustus undoubtedly glowed.

THE KING-ELECTOR'S GEOGRAPHY

George II Augustus followed his father in choosing London as his main *Residenz*, while ordaining that the electoral court in Hanover should be held in perpetual readiness. Whatever the contents of his father's will had been, they magnified his feelings of insecurity. Brunswick-Lüneburg was his backstop, his strategic Plan B. If ever the composite state faltered, he could always fall back on the family base.

As from June 1727, George Augustus, aged forty-three, was lord of the Electorate of Brunswick-Lüneburg centred on Hanover, of the dependent duchy of Saxe-Lauenberg administered from Ratzeburg near Lübeck, and of the twin duchies of Bremen and Verden, jointly run from Stade on the Elbe. The electoral territories in the *Unterwald*, including Hoya and Diepholz, had been consolidated; in the *Oberwald* they were split between Göttingen and Grubenhagen. The lakeside town of Ratzeburg (today in Schleswig-Holstein) lay close to the Baltic. The old *Hansehaven* at Stade – today a suburb of Greater Hamburg – provided access to the North Sea. The nearby district of Lüchow-Dannenberg, anciently settled by Slavs and known as the 'Hanoverian Wendland', was entering the terminal stage of assimilation.[8]

Travellers of the era, such as Baron von Pöllnitz, reported that Hanover was a bustling commercial city, adorned by fine red-brick churches and spacious squares.[9] The old ducal castle, the Leineschloss, was overshadowed by the splendours of Herrenhausen, whose French-style Baroque gardens – nowadays used by German chancellors to receive foreign dignitaries – were already famous for their resplendent tree-lined avenues and flower-beds and the gigantic fountain, boasting Europe's highest water plume.

The port city of Stade, beneath its massive Swedish-built fortress, was equally remarkable. Its customs station, the *Elbezoll*, took dues from every ship approaching or leaving Hamburg. Its prowess in music and philosophy was associated with Dietrich Buxtehude and Carsten Niebuhr. Together with its twin city of Verden-an-der-Aller, it functioned within its own personal union.[10]

The *Grafschaft* or county of Bentheim on the Dutch border was added to the king-elector's domains in 1753 in exchange for an emergency loan given to its previous owner. Its grand medieval castle overlooked the spa town of Bad Bentheim and its sulphurous springs. Its golden sandstone, *Bentheimer Gold*, was exported far and wide.[11]

George Augustus's Kingdom of Great Britain was still more complicated. Its two main parts, the conjoined Kingdoms of England and Scotland, remained distinct jurisdictions with strong national identities. There was a common royal government in London, a common British Parliament at Westminster, and unified armed forces. Wales was integrated with England and the Kingdom of Ireland was an English dependency. Wales, unindustrialized, was entering a Celtic revival. Ireland, ruled by an English lord lieutenant and by the parliament of the Protestant Anglo-Irish gentry, was plagued by discriminatory penal laws and run, like Guernsey, Jersey and the Isle of Man, as a Crown possession. There was no 'United Kingdom'; 'Britishness' was in its infancy.[12]

Despite forty-six years in the British Isles, George II Augustus never set foot in Ireland, Scotland or Wales, nor even in northern England, always keeping within reach of a ship to the continent. He took the waters at Bath, visited Oxford, Cambridge and the races at Newmarket, and stayed at aristocratic houses such as Blenheim, Stowe or Woburn. His one royal progress, undertaken as Prince of Wales, toured England's home counties. He never saw Georgian Edinburgh, Georgian Dublin or Georgian Cardiff.[13]

In London, the Tudor-built St James's Palace, containing the monarch's abode, the central offices and the premises of the court, had housed the royal headquarters since the great Whitehall fire of 1698. The presence of the *Deutsche Kanzlei* (German Chancery) made it the focus for electoral as well as royal business.

The royal City of Westminster stood apart physically and legally from the City of London. The Church of St Martin-in-the-Fields (1726) occupied the open space between them. The government district of Whitehall was divided off by the Holbein Gate from the parliamentary district around Westminster Hall and Westminster Abbey. George II Augustus oversaw the construction of the old Treasury (1737) and, replacing the former royal tiltyard, his beloved Horse Guards Parade. Before moving in permanently, he treated Kensington Palace, William III's home, as an alternative residence and riding lodge. Other palaces used included the Dutch House at Kew, Windsor Castle and Hampton Court. Greenwich was undergoing reconstruction.

The London which George Augustus knew was spreading on either bank of the Thames, its main waterborne thoroughfare. Freshly graced by Christopher Wren's fifty-one churches, and dominated by the colossal dome of St

Paul's Cathedral (1710), it was connected to the outside world by the wharves, piers and dockyards below the Tower. Mayfair and Covent Garden were new fashionable districts.

The eastern suburb of Spitalfields was home to a dynamic community of French Huguenot weavers.[14] Their Église de l'Hôpital (now the Brick Lane Mosque) opened in 1743, at a time when the Huguenots were producing an astonishing number of prominent Londoners. Claude Aymand (1660–1740) was the king-elector's principal surgeon,[15] David Garrick (De la Garrigue, 1717–79) his favourite actor and theatre manager;[16] Paul de Lamerie (1688–1751) his master silversmith;[17] and Abel Boyer (1667–1729) the author of his much-thumbed English-French dictionary.[18]

A rural setting surrounded Lord Burlington's magnificent Palladian villa at Chiswick House (1729). Montagu House, the first site of the British Museum (1753) stood on the city's northern perimeter. Popular recreational venues included Vauxhall Gardens and Tyburn Tree, 'God's tribunal', where public hangings were still staged. Among everyday dangers, smallpox, rabies, syphilis and gin topped the list, followed by press gangs, 'blacked-up' robbers, sedan chairs, debtors' prisons and the pestilential Fleet Ditch.[19]

There is one last telling detail. Before 1733, the 'House at the Back' on Cockpit Corner, later known as Downing Street, was occupied by Baron von Bothmer, the chief minister not of Great Britain but of Brunswick-Lüneburg.[20]

In 1727, Great Britain inherited a score of colonies in North America, the Caribbean and the Mediterranean[21] – a major source of Crown income – and controlled the

Hudson's Bay Company. George Washington (1732–99), born in Virginia, was named for the king-elector, who increased the colonial tally by three, carved two new colonies out of the Carolina Territory and, in 1732, commissioned General James Oglethorpe to found the colony of Georgia, also in his name.

James Oglethorpe (1696–1785), a former adjutant to Eugene of Savoy, an MP and a social reformer, devised the plan to make a new colony for destitute ex-sailors and debtors, free of class divisions, slavery and rum. Having obtained a royal charter for thirty years from George Augustus, he landed aboard HMS *Anne* with a cargo of settlers and cotton seed in December 1732, leased land from the Yamacraw Indians and founded Savannah. The king-elector personally received a delegation of Cherokees, and under Georgia's founding charter appointed four governors: James Oglethorpe (1732–43), William Stephens (1743–51), Henry Parker (1751–3) and Patrick Graham (1753–4).[22]

Military-style settlement floundered, however, and the chosen crops – vines, mulberry trees and cotton – proved unprofitable. As a result, the colony returned to royal administration for the rest of the reign as a 'royal province', when three more governors were appointed: John Reynolds (1754–7), Henry Ellis (1757–60) and Sir James Wright (1760–82). For the Georgian planters, the crucial issue was slave-holding; they saw themselves disadvantaged compared to South Carolina, whose Fundamental Constitutions, drawn up by the king-elector, fully endorsed slavery. So in 1749, Governor Stephens lifted the ban on importing slaves; the labour force increased; and before long, Governor

Wright was proclaiming Georgia to be 'the most flourishing colony on the continent'.[23]

THE COURT

The court of the sovereign was the beating heart of all European monarchies: in Boswell's words, 'the cause of so much show and splendour'. Modelled on Versailles, it was an arena where the monarch rose above all others, glorified and flattered by countless rituals and ceremonies.

British historians tend to stress that in early Georgian times 'the Monarchy was in decline' and 'slowly sinking in status',[24] implying that the court's glittering façade concealed a lesser reality. George Augustus might well have exploded at that sort of talk. Regardless of later developments, he and his entourage would have thought that the monarchy was pushing back against former limitations and that the court gave them a place for doing so. What is more, the royal and electoral court was not a purely British institution; under George Augustus it embodied the personal union joining Great Britain to the Electorate, encouraging British, Irish and Hanoverian nobles and officials to mix and mingle.

Traditionally, the court, which had itinerant origins, assembled wherever the monarch happened to be. The king-elector, when in London, convened it either at St James's Palace or increasingly at Kensington. Yet St James's, initially the main seat both of the sovereign's household and of court assemblies, was described by one courtier as 'crazy, smoky and dirty' and 'the contempt of foreign nations and the disgrace of our own',[25] and can hardly have matched George Augustus's dreams. It was crammed with a thousand servants of all ranks, ranging from grandees, such as the Lord Steward or Lord Chamberlain, to the rat-catchers and the 'necessary women', who collected and emptied the chamber pots. Like Versailles, which had tens of thousands of inhabitants and no toilets, it emitted a stench mitigated only by oceans of strong perfume. In addition to the sovereign's suite of chambers and the Grand Drawing Room, it housed both the German Chancery, from which the Electorate was governed, and the 'German Chapel' (as the Chapel Royal was then called), where Lutheran services were held.

The court assembled in a variety of modes. The king-elector held modest morning *levées*, usually for gentlemen only, and evening soirées for mixed company. Four times a week he presided over the full court in the Grand Drawing Room, where fashionable court dress was multicoloured and ostentatious to a fault. Men wore powdered periwig, frock coat, embroidered waistcoat, knee breeches, silken stockings, high-heeled shoes, bejewelled buckles and sword and sash, and carried a folded *chapeau-bras*. Over their tight-drawn stays and hooped petticoats women wore the long, Spanish-style *mantua*, replete with towering headdress, cascading ruffles and trailing train, augmented by 'rosy cheeks, snowy foreheads and bosoms, jet eyebrows and scarlet lips'.[26]

For, unlike Parliament, which was a wholly male preserve, the court provided the one arena where women came to see and be seen. In a rigidly patriarchal society women faced severe restrictions, and many had to imitate the queen-electress, 'who kept her husband subtly but firmly under her thumb'.[27] Others, who had accompanied George Augustus and Caroline from Leicester House, defied convention more openly. Mary Bellenden (1694–1736), now the Duchess of Argyll, and her long-term companion, Molly Lepell (1700–68), a German soldier's daughter and now Lady Hervey, did nothing to hide a racy past. For, notwithstanding the titles, 'the palace's most elegant assembly room was in fact a bloody battlefield. This was a world of skulduggery, politicking, wigs and beauty spots, where fans whistled open like flick-knives. Intrigue hissed through the crowd ... Beneath their powder and perfume, the courtiers stank of sweat, insecurity and glittering ambition.'[28]

Under George Augustus, the court factions gathered not only round partisan Whigs and Tories, but also round cliques of household officials or government ministers, round Scots and English, Britishers and Germans. Thanks to the interplay of the sexes, they were 'full of politics, anger, friendship, love, fucking and foppery', being also known as 'fuctions'.[29]

Above all, the court served as a grand stage for political theatre, where George Augustus could act out his sovereign's God-given role with panache. Whenever he entered, the entire company would bow low in obeisance, freezing their subservient position until the monarch graciously waved them to rise. As he sat enthroned, his courtiers sank to their knees and kissed his hand, hanging on his every word and gesture, looking to see who was welcomed and who shunned. 'The winners and losers ... could calculate precisely how far they'd climbed – or how low they'd fallen – by the warmth of their reception.'[30] These practices exuded a whiff of the absolutism which British law had supposedly curbed.

George Augustus possessed the means to reward and control the court nobility, and revelled in the pomp and invented traditions surrounding the chivalric orders. He regularly attended the annual June assemblies of the Order of the Garter at St George's Chapel, Windsor, and over the years invested thirty-one Garter Knights – the first being the Dukes of Cumberland, Chesterfield and Burlington in 1730 and the last the Prince of Brunswick-Bevern in 1759.[31] Without ever visiting Edinburgh, he created seventeen Knights of the Thistle, starting with the Duke of Tankerville in 1730 and ending with the 6th Duke of Hamilton in 1755.[32] As a Protestant he was excluded from the Empire's similar orders, so warmly welcomed England's pseudo-chivalric dramas.[33]

In those days, household and court officials enjoyed parity with government ministers, and George Augustus relied on them heavily. He was particularly indebted to Charles FitzRoy, Duke of Grafton (1683–1757), Lord Chamberlain under two reigns,[34] who was a generous patron of music, and from 1737 organizer of the office for the censorship of playhouses.[35] Continuity was also provided by the two Lords Berkeley of Stratton, father and son, who occupied a string of court posts.[36] Under the Lord Chamberlain, the most important household positions included the Vice-Chamberlain, the Treasurer of the Chamber, the Groom of the Stole, the Master of the Robes and the Keeper of the Privy Purse. The hierarchy of the Bedchamber put lords and gentlemen at the top and grooms and pages at the bottom. The king-elector's longest-serving servants were the bilingual Augustus Schütz, Keeper of the Purse 1727–57, and J. Ranby, for nearly forty years his Barber to the Person.[37]

Thanks to the growth of Cabinet government, the British Privy Council's role diminished. Yet the Council always met in the palace monthly, issuing Orders-in-Council. Three Lords President of the Council figured among George Augustus's closest advisers: the Earls of Wilmington (from 1730 to 1742) and of Granville (from 1751 to 1763), and the Duke of Dorset (from 1745 to 1751). Simultaneously, the king-elector took constant advice from the Electorate's Privy Council, headed from 1735 to 1753 by Heinrich, Baron Grote.

International diplomacy was a further key court function. All foreign diplomats were accredited not to the government but to 'the Court of St James'. Strictly speaking, they were not representatives of their country, but of one monarch to another, and by their bearing sought to express their masters' power and magnificence. Many, like Joachim Trotti, Marquis de la Chétardie or the Duc de Mirepoix from France or the Russian Ivan Andreevich Shcherbatov, were colourful and haughty grandees. Others, like Louis-Guy de Guérapin de Vauréal, Bishop of Rennes and member of the *Académie française*, were churchmen. During George Augustus's reign a score of permanent embassies functioned in London, from the French and the Imperial to the Saxon, the Swedish and the Prussian. Other monarchs sent special envoys on specific missions. One peculiarity was that the embassy chapels of Catholic countries acted as magnets for worshippers banned from practising in public elsewhere.

The Spanish and the Sardinian chapels were two such venues.[38]

The one thing *not* permitted was to defy the boycott on the Stuart Pretenders. In 1729, the plenipotentiary of the Duke of Parma was unceremoniously expelled from London because his master had invited the Old Pretender for a meeting in Italy.[39]

Extraordinarily, for forty-eight years (1710–58), one man, whom George Augustus met almost daily, held the key post of Master of Ceremonies to London's diplomatic corps, receiving the diplomats' letters of credence, hearing their reports, or bidding them farewell. Sir Clement Cottrell-Dormer (1686–1758), a well-known bibliophile, passed his position to his son when he died at the family estate of Rousham House near Oxford.[40]

RELIGION

George II Augustus was keenly aware that his royal advancement was entirely dependent on his Protestant credentials. Yet nothing indicates that he possessed a fervent sense of religious belief, or was awed by his responsibilities in the Church of England. He appears to have believed in vampires,[41] but the zeal of preceding times was abating, and a revered philosopher could write in deistic mode: 'If God were not to exist, he would have to be invented.' [42]

George II Augustus's homeland, the Holy Roman Empire, consisted of a patchwork of Catholic and Protestant states. Religious uniformity was still more or less enforced within each of them, but toleration practised between them. The king-elector's superior, the emperor, was a Catholic, while he himself belonged to the Protestant *Corpus Evangelicorum*; many relatives and neighbours were either Papists or Calvinists. He was accustomed to religious difference, if not necessarily to true tolerance.

Yet George Augustus, like his father, held a position that raised him above the rank and file. As the *Summus Episcopus* of the Electorate's Lutheran Church, he followed an Anglican-style practice which combined ecclesiastical with secular functions,[43] preparing him well for the set-up which he met in England. There are no signs that he suffered pangs of conscience when becoming the Church of England's Supreme Governor and the *Summus Episcopus* simultaneously.

Religious practice within Brunswick-Lüneburg revealed a patchwork within patchworks. Historically, the religious centre lay at Hildesheim, some eighteen miles from Hanover, where St Gotthard's shrine drew pilgrims to its Benedictine abbey. At the Reformation, the majority of the population had followed their dukes into Lutheranism, but the prince-bishopric of Hildesheim remained a self-ruling Catholic enclave. From 1723 to 1761 its prince-bishop was an ecclesiastical pluralist, Clemens-August von Bayern (1700–61), a Wittelsbach. In one of his other capacities, as Archbishop of Cologne, Clemens-August crowned his brother, Charles VII, at Frankfurt in 1742.[44]

The Saxon city of Halle, just over the border from Brunswick-Lüneburg, was another significant religious centre. Closely connected to Luther's birthplace at nearby Wittenberg, the University of Halle, founded in 1694, was famed for its pursuit of non-sectarian academic freedom and of Pietism, an austere and widespread brand of Lutheranism which would influence the ideas of John Wesley in England.[45]

Hanover city was religiously compartmentalized. The city council and ducal establishment were strictly Protestant. Catholics and Jews were excluded from the *Altstadt*, though one Catholic church and one synagogue functioned in the *Neustadt* across the river.

On moving to London, George Augustus found that the British Isles formed yet another religious patchwork. Great Britain's southern part was subject to the established Church of England, the northern part to the Presbyterian Church of Scotland. The Anglican Church of Ireland enjoyed state-backed privileges, defying the Catholic faith of most Irish people. Everywhere, religious worship was controlled by a variety of monopolies, restrictions and penal laws. In England, Roman Catholics, Nonconformists and Jews were permitted to worship but not to study at university or to hold public office. Within the clergy, after decades of dissension, the spirit of trimming was rife. It was epitomized by the semi-legendary Vicar of Bray, immortalized in a song from the 1720s:

> The illustrious House of Hanover and Protestant Succession:
> To these I do allegiance swear, while they can keep possession.
> For in my faith and loyalty I never more will falter,
> And George my lawful king shall be, until the times do alter.
> And this is law that I'll maintain until my dying day, Sir,
> That whatsoever king may reign I'll be the Vicar of Bray, Sir.[46]

George Augustus kept clear of contemporary religious movements, though several enjoyed substantial support. Latitudinarianism, which sought the *via media* between Protestants and Catholics, condemned doctrinaire attitudes; Arminianism had taken hold in the Netherlands as a liberal reaction to the Calvinist concept of predestination. The youngest movement, later labelled Methodism, was coalescing in Oxford around the Wesley brothers and their friend George Whitefield (1714–70), as the new reign opened. John Wesley (1703–91), ordained an Anglican priest in 1728, was to travel 250,000 miles on horseback, preaching 40,000 sermons and leading a country-wide religious revival. Charles Wesley (1707–88), composed over 6,000 incomparable hymns, including 'Jesus, Lover of my Soul' and 'Love Divine':

> Love Divine, all loves excelling,
> Joy of Heaven to earth come down,
> Fix in us Thy humble dwelling,
> All Thy faithful Mercies crown
> Jesus, Thou art all compassion,
> Pure unbounded love Thou art;
> Visit us with Thy salvation,
> Enter every trembling heart.[47]

George Augustus's predicament in all of this was not enviable. He, a non-Anglican and leader of a foreign religious denomination, was anointed 'Defender of the Faith', 'Supreme Governor' of the Anglican Church, 'God's Vice-regent on Earth' and the formal mediator between God and man. '*Rex Angliae est Persona Mixta cum Sacerdote*,' wrote

Chamberlayne, 'as it were a Priest as well as a King . . . his Person is Sacred and Spiritual'.[48] Somehow, the recipient of these favours took it all in his stride, performing his duties as directed by churchmen and making no public comment. His task was greatly eased by the absence of the Church of England's assembly, the Convocation, which his father had suspended in 1717 and which would not reconvene until 1852.[49] In other circumstances, he could have been struggling to deal with the Convocation's warring houses, where the laity habitually attacked the bishops. As it was, he could rule the Church calmly and without interference, assisted only by a well-tamed clerical hierarchy.

After Archbishop Wake's death, the king-elector appointed four Anglican primates: John Potter (r. 1737–47), a theologian, and three former royal chaplains – the loyalist and Latitudinarian Thomas Herring (r. 1747–57), Matthew Hutton (r. 1757–8), a former Bishop of Bangor, and Thomas Secker (r. 1758–68), sometime Nonconformist and Bishop of Oxford. Another prominent prelate, Lancelot Blackburne (1658–1743), who gained high preferment despite his former career as a pirate, epitomized the high clergy's notoriously louche lifestyle, which so infuriated the revivalists. 'The jolly old Archbishop of York', wrote Horace Walpole, 'retained nothing of his old profession except his seraglio.'[50]

As head of two episcopalian Churches, George Augustus had no special brief for Nonconformity. But neither did he impede the Nonconformists' steady progress towards general acceptance. In Scotland, he was sworn to uphold the establishment of the national Presbyterian Church. In England, many dissenters like Joseph Priestley (1733–1804) were influenced by rationalism and scientific thinking. The King's Head Society, dating from 1731, contributed to the rapid spread and high reputation of dissenting academies.[51]

Like Hanover, London sheltered a small Jewish community, which clustered round the Bevis Marks synagogue near Aldgate – officially the Kahal Khadosz Shaar Asamaim, or 'Holy Congregation of the Heavenly Gates'. Its Sephardi members, mainly Anglo-Spanish merchants, were nominally subject to the ancient *De Judaismo* Statute, requiring them to wear 'Jew badges'. Under George Augustus they included Benjamin Mendes de Costa, who bought out the synagogue's freehold in 1747; Benjamin D'Israeli (1730–1816), the future prime minister's grandfather, who arrived from Italy in 1748; and the Abudiente family, who had changed their name to Gideon. Sampson Abudiente Gideon (1699–1762), son of a sugar planter from Barbados, was reputedly the wealthiest among them. Well acquainted with Robert Walpole and the Duke of Newcastle, and presumably with George Augustus, he was 'one of the most famous financiers of his day', who invested in landed estates near Spalding in Lincolnshire. By 1759, he was able to obtain a baronetcy for his fourteen-year-old son, the future Lord Eardley, an Eton schoolboy suitably instructed in the Anglican faith.[52]

'When [George II Augustus] ascended the throne', states an old history, 'the Church of England reposed in tranquillity,' while also asserting: 'Real piety experienced a melancholy decline and licentiousness overspread the land.'[53] The tranquillity was only relative. Anglican divines queued up to denounce everything from deism, gin and the theatre to

Wesley's theology and David Hume's philosophy. Furious flurries of religious tracts and pamphlets flew back and forth. '[The Archbishop]', observed George Whitefield, 'knew no more of Christianity than Mahomet.' 'Methodism and Popery are closely allied,' came the response. Selina Hastings, Countess of Huntingdon (1707–91) championed the revivalists.[54] The Roman Catholic Richard Challoner (1691–1781), author of *Britannia Sancta*, bravely attacked Protestant myths.[55] The outspoken Bishop of Winchester, Benjamin Hoadly (1676–1761), who had once proposed an Anglo-Scottish Church union, battled the High Church Tories.[56] William Whiston (1667–1752), mathematician, popular theologian and a self-declared Arian, began as an expellee from Cambridge and ended as a Baptist.[57] Literary churchmen like Thomas Sherlock, Bishop of London (1678–1761) and William Warburton, Bishop of Gloucester (1698–1779) held the middle ground. Amid the clamour, George Augustus must have smiled on hearing he was 'the new King David'.[58] He promoted Archbishop Herring following a sermon in 1747 stating: 'We are now blessed with the mild administration of a Just and Protestant King.'[59]

No evidence links the king-elector with Freemasonry, though several leading courtiers, including his Earl Marshal, the 8th Duke of Norfolk (1683–1732), acted as Grand Master of England's Grand Lodge. During his reign, the movement expanded to many British cities and also to Paris, Berlin and St Petersburg.[60] In 1744 George Augustus personally intervened to obtain the release in Lisbon of John Coustos (1703–46), a Freemason and alleged spy of Robert Walpole, who had been captured and tortured by the Inquisition.[61]

Voltaire stayed in London from 1726 to 1729. 'An Englishman, as one to whom liberty is natural,' he wrote, 'may go to heaven his own way.'[62] George Augustus would have said 'Amen' to that. For arguably the decline of bigotry and enforced uniformity was giving him a welcome political dividend. In the previous century, it had been the supercharged fears of Roman Catholicism which drove Parliament's limitation of royal power in the Glorious Revolution. The fading of those fears gave the king-elector a margin for manoeuvre, whereby he and his ministers could quietly recover lost ground. The absence of anything worse than noisy pamphlet wars created the opportunity to manage Parliament from above, and to stem attacks on the monarchy.

ECONOMY

During the decades preceding his reign, George Augustus saw the economic resources of his family possessions increase exponentially. In 1698, when the 'Hanoverian Project' was first mooted, the duchy of Calenberg was still separate from Celle. Twenty-nine years later, he was ruler not only of a greatly expanded Electorate but also of two, still larger insular kingdoms and their dependencies. Opinions differed as to what exactly constituted his 'possessions'; he would almost certainly have seen things differently from his British ministers. Even so, while bound by the law, and restrained by practicalities, he clearly expected that the resources of all his realms should contribute to the safety and prosperity of the whole.

Though *The Wealth of Nations* (1776) belonged to a

later generation, Adam Smith (1723–90) was the product of fermenting economic thought under George II Augustus; his *Theory of Moral Sentiments* was published in 1759. Conventional wisdom still supported the conviction that a good prince practised the same patient husbandry as a prudent nobleman; gradual 'improvement' rather than innovation was in fashion. Yet new ideas were brewing. The Irishman Richard Cantillon (1680–1734), for example, of whom George Augustus would have heard, had specialized in money transfers and in trading shares in John Law's Mississippi Company. Settling in England, he produced a treatise, the *Essai Sur la nature du commerce en général* (1730), which analysed monetary theory and spatial economics and is now seen as an essential prelude to Adam Smith and the French physiocrats; he coined the term of *entrepreneur* or 'risk-taker'.[63] Other pioneers were Jakob Bielfeld (1717–70), the inventor of 'political arithmetic' who once worked in the Prussian consulate in Hanover, and Gottfried Achenwall (1719–72), professor at Göttingen from 1748, and (in the German view) the 'father of statistics'.[64]

George Augustus and his milieu were more accustomed to entrusting the financial and economic business of state to a *Hoffaktor* or *Kammeragent*, commonly known as the *Hofjude* or 'court Jew'. His father and grandfather had relied on the banker Leffmann Behrens (1630–1714), founder of Hanover's *Neustadt* synagogue, who financed the Calenbergs' campaign to obtain electoral status. For forty years from 1726, the Electorate's financial affairs were run by Jakob Wolf Oppenheimer, grandson of the

Habsburgs' *Hofjude*, Samuel Oppenheimer. Several such court Jews met a bad end, but not in Hanover. From 1757 to 1763, Meyer Amschel Rothschild, founder of the banking dynasty, served his apprenticeship under J. W. Oppenheimer.[65]

Hanover's ruling circles could not fail to notice the policies of the Hohenzollerns, who were building the foundations of military power by economic means. Brandenburg-Prussia's natural resources were less than Brunswick's, but nimble management in Berlin was producing results. Skilled migrants were welcomed. Manufactures were developed. The famous Prussian excise boosted revenues. And in fifty years, the size of the army quadrupled. Aided by his Chief Factor, Daniel Itzig (1723–99), the king-elector's nephew, Frederick, assembled the era's most sensational military machine.

In Hanover, as elsewhere, the profitable business of hiring out mercenary soldiers was thriving. The upkeep of costly military establishments could be offset, when convenient, by leasing out officers, technical experts or whole regiments. George Augustus's neighbour and relative, the Landgrave of Hesse-Kassel, was the trade's leading exponent. The king-elector would have thought it entirely normal that Hanoverian regiments should be hired out for cash to the British service.

In Great Britain, George II Augustus was surrounded by courtier-landowners for whom agricultural improvement was staple talk. Foremost among them was Walpole's brother-in-law, Charles, Viscount Townshend (1674–1738). A former ambassador, 'Turnip Townshend' ran British foreign policy as secretary of state before retiring in 1730 to his estate at

Raynham Hall in Norfolk, where he perfected the four-course system of crop rotation, greatly increasing both cereal yields and the supply of fresh meat.[66] Two other names were on everyone's lips: that of the well-travelled Oxfordshire farmer Jethro Tull (1674–1741), inventor of the seed-drill, author of *Horse-hoeing Husbandry* (1731), and the father of mechanized agriculture,[67] and that of Robert Bakewell (1725–95), the revolutionary horse and livestock breeder from Leicestershire. George Augustus, too, excelled in horse-breeding. In 1735 he founded the State Stud at Celle, which launched the Hanoverian horse, the most successful warm-blood breed of all time.[68]

Improvers, however, could do damage. In 1756, the Earl of Harcourt demolished the village of Nuneham Courtenay in Oxfordshire to make way for his Palladian villa, inspiring a famous poem lamenting 'Old England's demise':

> Ill fares the land, to hast'ning ills a prey,
> Where wealth accumulates and men decay;
> Princes and lords may flourish, or may fade –
> A breath can make them, as a breath has made –
> But a bold peasantry, their country's pride,
> When once destroy'd can never be supplied.[69]

Three years later, work began in Lancashire on the Bridge-water Canal, linking the estate of Francis Egerton, Duke of Bridgewater (1736–1803) with his coal mines at Worsley. It made the duke the richest nobleman in England, and symbolizes the onset of the Industrial Revolution, with all its benefits and evils.

The Industrial Revolution, however, was building on

foundations laid by the pre-existing world of early capitalist commerce and finance – a world perfectly familiar to George Augustus. The king-elector, having served as Governor of the South Sea Company for a total of thirty-six years, was a major stakeholder in the strategic arrangement whereby the ruling family joined the Whigs in controlling the nexus between government and finance. The company's headquarters at South Sea House on Threadneedle Street lay in the heart of the City, alongside the Bank of England, the Royal Exchange, the East India Company and Lloyd's. After the Bubble of 1720, it abandoned its original trading brief and plunged into a variety of high-level financial operations. In those circumstances, it was hardly conceivable that the company's chief patron was *not* introduced to the wheelers and dealers of nearby Exchange Alley, stockbrokers like Sampson Gideon, who ran the high-risk sector of speculation, shady investment and emergency loans. A near-contemporary described Sampson Gideon admiringly: 'a Jew Broker, the most considerable of his Tribe, the Great Oracle . . . of Jonathan's Coffee House in Exchange-alley . . . and the Great Agent and Manager . . . of Ready-money Fortunes. He amassed a very considerable property . . . but was a man of strong natural understanding, of great liberality and generosity, and of some fun and humour.'[70]

The Bank of England had been founded in 1694, but most financial transactions still took place in specie, and George II Augustus was well used to seeing coins bearing his name and bust. Brunswick-Lüneburg minted bronze, silver and gold coins, starting with the simple 1 *Pfennig Scheide Munz* and rising to the magnificent 1 *Goldgulden*.

(In Lower Saxon currency, 1 *Thaler* = 24 *Groschen* = 36 *Mariengroschen* = 288 *Pfennigs*; 1 *Goldgulden* = 1.5 *Thaler*.) Inscriptions celebrated GEORGIUS DUX BR&LUN REX MB, HIB, FR. Designs included the Brunswick horse, the royal arms and the giant '*Wilder Mann*' with loincloth and sapling club.[71]

In Great Britain, the Royal Mint issued copper, silver and gold money, from 1 farthing to 5 guineas, based on the equivalence of 1 guinea = 21 shillings: 1 pound = 4 crowns = 20 shillings = 240 pence = 960 farthings. Designs evolved from the early-Roman-style 'armoured bust' to the 'old bust' of 1755.[72] So-called 'regal coppers', sporting a crowned harp, were used in Ireland.[73]

Masses of financial accounts survive in the Royal Archives, as do widespread rumours of George Augustus being the miserly royal Scrooge of British History. One surprising source suggests that the characterization may be true; the king-elector, it seems, was immortalized in a marvellously enigmatic nursery rhyme, first printed in London in *Tommy Thumb's Pretty Song Book* in 1744:

> Sing a song of sixpence,
> A pocketful of rye.
> Four and twenty blackbirds,
> Baked in a pie.
>
> When the pie was opened,
> The birds began to sing;
> Wasn't that a dainty dish,
> To set before the king?

The king was in his counting house,
Counting out his money;
The queen was in the parlour,
Eating bread and honey.

The maid was in the garden,
Hanging out the clothes;
When down came a blackbird
And pecked off her nose.[74]

Given the publication date, it is hard to dismiss the idea that the image of a monarch 'counting out his money' does indeed refer to George Augustus. And the idea is supported by what we know of his frugality. The king-elector built nothing for himself comparable to the grandiose edifices of his chief ministers, whether at Schloss Bothmer or Holkham Hall. But he ended his reign, exceptionally, with his counting house filled with £100,000 in savings.

SOCIETY

For George Augustus and his family, social status represented the most important feature of their lives. The two key life-changing events of their careers occurred in 1692, when they moved up into the highest rank of German princes, and in 1714, when they entered the still more select company of European royalty. Thereafter, they assiduously exploited the royal brand. Whether or not George Augustus truly believed in the divine origins of his advancement, *Deo Gratia*, is open to question. But, driven no doubt by the need to outbid the exiled Stuarts, he demanded and received lavish shows of deference, putting a clear distance between himself and the grandest magnates. In the rigid hierarchies of pre-industrial society, determined by lands and titles, he stood at the pinnacle. To his mind, *primus inter pares* hardly described his exalted position.

As a youthful soldier, George Augustus would have seen himself in the chivalric tradition, upholding the socio-political order sword in hand; but as an Imperial officer, he could have gasped at the social gap separating the Guelphs from the Habsburgs. He grew up among a cluster of extremely ambitious German princes, all with royal aspirations. By 1727, no less than eight of George Augustus's princely neighbours were enjoying, or had enjoyed, royal status, namely: Christian V and Frederick IV of Oldenburg, Kings of Denmark (r. 1670–1730), Charles XI, Charles XII and Ulrike Eleonora from the house of the Palatinate-Zweibrücken, sovereign rulers of Sweden (r. 1660–1720), Frederick William I, King of Prussia (r. 1713–40), August II of Saxony (der Starke), King of Poland (r. 1697–1733), and Frederick of Hesse-Kassel, King of Sweden (r. 1720–51). Nonetheless, after mounting the British throne he was closing the gap. He had joined the super-elite, who had all secured their badge of royalty.[75] For him, this German context exerted an importance which few Britishers appreciated.

The king-elector's understanding of the social order was formed by conditions experienced in his early years in Brunswick-Lüneburg. His electoral subjects were disciplined, God-fearing and surprisingly well educated, but well over half of them were serfs, legally tied to the land. Serfdom was to survive in Germany into the next century, cementing immobile modes of thought and the gulf between the free and the unfree. The nobles, the clergy and the burghers enjoyed distinct rights and liberties. Yet most peasants were forbidden to leave their villages, or, under pain of fierce punishments, to disobey their masters' commands.[76] And George Augustus, owner of numerous ducal estates, was the greatest serf master in the land. His bloated sense of social self-importance was unparalleled in Britain, except perhaps by colonial slave masters.

Within the Electorate, the Guelphs had no equals. Barons, *Landgrafen* (landgraves) and *Freiherren* (barons) abounded; the families of von Kielmansegg, von Görtz, von Ilten, von Bothmer or von Münchhausen possessed ancestral lands, castles, manors and serfs. But they were all the king-elector's subjects and inferiors.[77]

In addition to Hanover, George Augustus's Electorate contained a dozen notable cities, each with its charter and liberties. Celle differed from Stade, and Hamelin from Ratzeburg. All had their ruined medieval walls, their market square, their town hall and their church. Nowadays they are listed on Germany's *Fachwerkstrasse*, the 'Timber-frame Road'. The city freemen, organized into powerful craft guilds and serving as elected councillors and *Bürgermeister*, were a caste apart from both nobles and peasants.[78]

None was prouder of its traditions than the former Hanse city of Göttingen, much favoured by George Augustus. Located on the upper Leine, it had long contested the rival claims of Calenberg and Wolfenbüttel, before joining

the Electorate definitively in 1692.[79] The king-elector pre-
pared to found the University of Göttingen, the 'Georgina
Augusta', from the outset.

Social conditions in early Georgian Great Britain were
markedly more fluid than in the Electorate. Feudalism – if
ever a reality – had disappeared long ago, and informal
socio-economic classes were the norm. Yet, though out-
numbered in the countryside by the gentry and by sturdy
yeoman farmers, the landed aristocracy retained its dom-
inance. The merchants were as wealthy and numerous as in
any European country. Rural tenant farmers were pressur-
ized by the relentless spread of enclosures. Continental-style
peasants, subsistence farmers, were only represented by the
crofters of marginal land, especially in the 'Celtic fringe'.

The king-elector's personal involvement with British
society was largely confined to the peerage, who surrounded
him in court and government circles. By 1727, as consolidated in the House of Lords, the British peerage included
eighteen dukes, five marquises, sixty-eight earls, eight viscounts and fifty-eight barons – 157 in total. Peacock-proud
of their seniority, they were headed by the English Dukes of
Norfolk and Bedford, and the Scottish Dukes of Hamilton
and Argyll.[80]

In the social politics of the reign, the king-elector's crucial
powers of patronage were skilfully exercised through a strategy of holding the peerage in loyal expectation. In thirty-three
years, he created no dukedoms and only two baronies and
nine earldoms. John Monson, commissioner for trade and
plantations, elevated in 1728, was the first to receive a barony. The freshly promoted earls ranged from Waldegrave

(1729), Wilmington (1730) and Orford (1742) to Guildford (1752), Hardwicke (1754) and Warwick (1759).

Remarkably, neither of the two most distinguished British prime ministers of the age, Robert Walpole and William Pitt, actively sought a peerage. Walpole only accepted the earldom of Orford on his resignation. Pitt long prized the epithet of 'the Great Commoner', not becoming the Earl of Chatham until after George Augustus's death.

The Newcastles, in contrast, boosted by the merger of the Holles and Pelham families, had received their dukedom in 1715. Thomas Pelham-Holles (1693–1768), Duke of Newcastle upon Tyne of Claremont House in Surrey, was the ultimate political insider. In 1756, George Augustus mischievously awarded him the additional dukedom of Newcastle-under-Lyne.[81]

The rigid socio-political system, which the Newcastles epitomized, was laid bare 200 years later by the prosopographic method of Lewis Namier. Prosopography analyses social groups by tracing family connections, networks of patronage, patterns of office-holding and sources of income. Applied to mid-eighteenth-century parliamentarians, it undermined the older Whig Interpretation of Georgian history, which emphasized party rivalries. Namier's *The Structure of Politics at the Accession of George III* (1929), a scholarly milestone, summarized the outcome of developments under George II Augustus, which included vast corruption and the subordination of Parliament to the monarchy.[82]

The king-elector must have blinked at the rapidly expanding City of London, which was larger than all the Electorate's cities combined. Its port, handling 50,000 ships per year, put Hamburg or Bremen into the shade. Its social life, thronged with merchants, bankers and globetrotting seamen, was unique. Its municipal autonomy was respected by George Augustus, who happily attended the Lord Mayor's parades.[83]

Naturally, Georgian society had its seamier side, in which some courtiers wallowed. Frances Dashwood, Baron Despencer (1708–81), notorious rake and leader of the Hellfire Club, organized uninhibited orgies in his caves at West Wycombe.[84] London's sex trade flourished blatantly. Harris's annual *List of Covent-Garden Ladies* detailed the professionals' specialities. '"Days of ease and nights of pleasure" is a motto this lewd girl never means to depart from,' it said of 'Miss T-m-s of 28, Frith Street, Soho'. 'We would advise the hero ... to plunge the carnal sword into its favourite scabbard.'[85]

One of the occasions when George Augustus encountered 'impolite society' occurred in Kensington Gardens. He was accosted by a highwayman, who 'with great deference' 'deprived [him] of his purse, his watch and his buckles'.[86]

Though no great philanthropist, George Augustus was personally involved in one of the world's first incorporated charities. In 1735, he received a petition from Thomas Coram (1668–1751), a former sea captain and American colonist, who had persuaded twenty-one aristocratic ladies to help establish a Foundling Hospital for abandoned children. Two years later, another petition arrived from the ladies' male relatives. The hospital's founding charter was issued in 1739, appointing Handel as governor.[87]

George II Augustus took charge of Great Britain in the

era when colonial slavery was rife and British ships took the lead in the Atlantic slave trade. Controlling the so-called 'Middle Passage' was a central issue in the Anglo-Spanish wars. No biographer has yet examined the extent of the king-elector's involvement or suggested that he personally managed the financing or regulation of slaving – as some of his predecessors undoubtedly did. The subject obviously requires research. Yet some facts speak for themselves. George Augustus joined the South Sea Company, and bought into its shares, at the exact time when it became the government's chosen instrument for exploiting the *Asiento de negros* and when slave-trading was its principal activity. He returned to the company's governorship on his father's death in 1727, and held the position through decades when slavery was never far from its remit. In the colonial sphere, he signed off the Statutes of Carolina, where slavery was a staple, altered the governance of Georgia to facilitate slavery, and inherited the position of chief patron to the Royal Africa Company, which never left the slaving sector. During his reign the British share of the slave trade was rising to 50,000 human beings per year. In 1750, the Royal Africa Company was dissolved by Act of Parliament and replaced by the government-backed African Company of Merchants, which, dealing in gold, guns and slaves, owned the principal West African slave-trading posts, including its headquarters at Cape Coast Castle in modern Ghana. The ACM's committee, consisting of representatives from London, Bristol and Liverpool, reported directly to the royal Exchequer, apparently indifferent to an average mortality rate of up to 20 per cent inflicted during the company's slaving voyages.[88] The early fortunes of Manchester were built on the slave-packed bales of slave-picked American cotton.[89] Several of the monarch's intimate associates, such as Charles Hayes, CEO of the ACM, or Viscount Deerhurst circulated in slavery-related commercial circles. Everything points to the likelihood that the monarch, if not a vocal advocate or instigator, was a complicit patron and un-protesting beneficiary.

What George Augustus thought about this human traf-ficking was not recorded. He must surely have heard tales like those from the early life of John Newton (1725–1807), the author of 'Amazing Grace', who was press-ganged into the Royal Navy during his reign, personally enslaved in Africa, and eventually converted to the cause of abolition, but only after a career as the foul-mouthed captain of slave ships.[90] In all probability, he looked on these established features of the age conventionally, as on the serfdom of his native Electorate, as part of the immutable social order 'which the Lord hath made'. He certainly did nothing to stop them. The sad truth may be, as one historian put it, that slavers 'in the England of [George II Augustus] were socially respectable'.[91] And it might help to explain the king-elector's great popularity among American colonists.

5
Head of the Family Firm

George Augustus's view of the 'family' was entirely dynastic. He had learned by hard experience that the happiness of individuals or the harmony between parents and children counted for less than the collective vigour of the family 'Firm'. As a member of Europe's super-elite of royals, he understood that the British Establishment, by settling the succession on his grandmother, had co-opted not just one person but the whole damn clan from Brunswick-Lüneburg-Calenberg, now magically morphed into 'the Hanoverians'. In response to British criticism, he could have retorted: 'The choice was yours!' Indeed, he would have given short shrift to talk of limitations to his sovereign power beyond those expressly embodied in British law. There was nothing in the Act of Settlement to prevent him holding non-British titles; and, as he saw it, his position as prince-elector at the head of the Calenberg Guelphs carried rights and duties, no less sacred than those derived from his tenure of the British crown.

Furthermore, his bitter feud with his father can only have increased both his sense of injustice and his appreciation of remaining relatives. He had lost his beloved grandparents long ago, and, seven months before his accession, his maltreated mother, unseen for over thirty years.[1] As is known from Henrietta Howard, when George Augustus moved into his father's premises at St James's Palace, the very first thing he did was to hang a portrait of his mother in the ante-chamber. Yet by 1727, his only blood relative still around was Charlotte, Viscountess Howe (1703–82), daughter of his aunt, Sophia von Kielmansegg, and wife of a former British minister in Hanover. Charlotte's three sons would serve in the top ranks either of the British army or the Royal Navy; her reward was a handsome annuity.[2]

Fortunately, George Augustus's marriage to Caroline of Ansbach was weathering the storms; the pair formed a close-knit team. Caroline did much more than bear their children. She was a close confidante and a true soulmate, supporting her husband in his quarrels, suffering his short-comings and restraining his impulses. She shared his low opinion of their eldest son, raised the cultural profile of his court, and guided him through many political thickets. Quite properly, his reign can be divided into the years with Caroline, and the longer span without her.

The balladeers, however, spared no one's blushes:

> You may strut, dapper George, but 'twill all be in vain;
> We know 'tis Queen Caroline, not you, doth reign.
> You govern no more than Don Philip of Spain.
> Then if you would have us fall down and adore you,
> Lock up your fat spouse, as your dad did before you.[3]

The verse was hinting at the widespread belief, that, while the queen-electress held the reins, 'dapper George' occupied himself with the minutiae – signing his papers, counting his money and drilling his soldiers. One can equally see a trusting couple working in unison. When in Germany, George Augustus wrote her copious weekly letters. Caroline, he felt, was well equipped to offer advice on princely politics. In one view, notwithstanding his infidelities, he remained 'emotionally faithful'.

Not that George Augustus was the easiest man to live with; the royal and electoral family enjoying an outing made quite a picture:

> His Majesty stayed about five minutes in the gallery: snubbed the Queen who was drinking chocolate, for being always stuffing: the Princess Emily for not hearing him: the Princess Caroline for being grown fat: the Duke of Cumberland for standing awkwardly: Lord Hervey for not knowing what relation the Prince of Sulzbach was to the Elector Palatine, and then carried the Queen to walk, and be re-snubbed, in the garden.[4]

The paterfamilias readily found fault with all and sundry, unable to win the children's confidence.[5]

Another snapshot is more sympathetic: 'In the drawing room he is gracious . . . to the ladies, and remarkably cheerful . . . His conversation is very proper for a tête à tête. He talks freely on most subjects, and very much to the purpose, but he cannot discourse with the same ease . . . in larger company.'[6] And there were moments when family life could look positively idyllic:

> The courtier Sir John Evelyn, grandson of the celebrated diarist, described how on 1st January 1729, he heard 'musick

and song performed in the Council Chamber, the King, Queen and Royal Family being in the great drawing roome with ye Company to hear them'. At the Prince's birthday several weeks later, Evelyn attended a sumptuous evening ball 'which his Royal Highness began by dancing a minuet with his eldest sister, the Princess Royal, after which French dances [were] held from ten to twelve, when country dances succeeded'.[7]

The key to the monarch's personality may lie in his military training. He could relax in set situations requiring little social agility, but reverted to type in front of perceived subordinates. '[He] judged the merit of all people', observed Lady Mary Wortley Montagu, 'by the ready submission to his orders.'[8] Neither his wife nor his ministers were spared. Above all, he adhered to an old-fashioned code of soldierly honour, which once led him, madly, to challenge the King of Prussia to a duel. This last incident, which occurred during the king-elector's visit to Hanover in 1729, seems to have tottered on the brink of disaster. George Augustus had ordered the arrest on electoral territory of a Prussian army press gang. Frederick William responded by arresting some stray Hanoverian haymakers, and by massing troops on the frontier. The duel was apparently fixed to take place at Hildesheim; George Augustus named Brigadier-General Richard Sutton, the British envoy to Hesse-Kassel, as his second; and diplomats struggled for months to cancel it. But the prospect of two European monarchs clashing in mortal combat seems not to have been totally unreal.[9]

George Augustus routinely took mistresses, giving them

honoured positions, some in London and others in reserve at Hanover – a good Anglo-German mix, reputedly humoured with sweepstake coupons. The first *maîtresse-en-titre*, Henrietta Howard, Countess of Suffolk, withdrew in 1734 with a handsome pay-off, from which she built Marble Hill Hall at Twickenham, remarried, ran a prominent salon and was eternalized by Alexander Pope (1688–1744):

> I know the thing that's most uncommon;
> (Envy be silent and attend!)
> I know a Reasonable Woman,
> Handsome and witty, yet a Friend.[10]

After a short interval, on Walpole's advice, Princess Amelia's governess, Lady Mary Deloraine (1703–44), stepped into Henrietta's shoes. She, too, suffered the monarch's snubs. According to Lord Hervey, 'His Majesty said that she stank unbearably of Spanish wine.' According to Walpole, she was 'a lying bitch'. 'People must wear old gloves,' he told Amelia, 'till they can get new ones.'[11]

The heir apparent, Friedrich von Welf (1707–51), variously known as 'Fred' or 'Griff', moved to London in 1728 aged twenty-one. Long separated from his parents on his grandfather's orders, he was hell-bent on a payback. Though loaded with British titles, including Prince of Wales, Duke of Edinburgh, and Baron of Snaudon, he preferred to be addressed as Prince Friedrich Ludwig of Hanover, joined the Freemasons, and kept his own wealthy and louche company, such as the 'indefatigable schemer', George Bubb Dodington (1691–1762).[12] He womanized wildly, sowing the royal and electoral seed with abandon. He shared a lover, Anne Vane, with Lord Hervey, and fathered a short-lived son, FitzFrederick Vane, born in 1732. He endlessly demanded money from his parents, and spiked their plans for his marriage. Via Dodington, he asked Parliament for increased funds behind their backs and sent secret emissaries to Berlin, where his parents were still hoping to keep their matrimonial scheme afloat.[13] He was behaving even worse than his father at the same age. His mother Caroline said that 'he looked like a frog', and was 'the greatest ass, the greatest liar, the greatest canaille, and the greatest beast in the world'.[14]

George Augustus was understandably angered, but might conceivably have handled his son better. He could have cosied up to the boy to suggest that they were both victims of the same old perpetrator. Instead, he allowed the intergenerational cycle of bad blood to fester. Caroline shared his outrage. Family harmony was absent during her lifetime.

George Augustus, however, kept his appetite. With teams of chefs on hand, he was accustomed to gargantuan meals, especially of meat and cakes. At one Christmas dinner he consumed plates of grilled capon, cold turkey, mutton and mince pies, before sitting down at supper to oysters in lemon, spinach and eggs, herring salad and frogs. Surviving menus from 1736–7 list pineapples, puffins, frogs and songbirds.[15]

And 'dapper George' lived up to his epithet. He often posed for painters in full regalia, appeared at court or theatre in grand outfits and outsize wigs, and loved military uniform.[16] At Prince Frederick's marriage in 1736 to the seventeen-year-old Princess Augusta of Saxe-Gotha, 'His Majesty was dressed in gold brocade turned up with silk, embroidered with large flowers in silver and colours, as was his waistcoat; the buttons and star were diamonds. Her Majesty was in plain yellow silk, laced with pearls, diamonds, and other [valuable] jewels.'

The family feud paused briefly for the wedding. The king-elector had earlier travelled from Hanover to Gotha, as he had once travelled to Ansbach, to inspect the prospective bride in person. Of Augusta, Caroline exclaimed: 'Poor Creature ! Were she to spit in my face, I should only pity her for being under the direction of such a fool.'

Matters came to a head after Frederick's parents discovered that he was concealing his wife's pregnancy. As head of the dynasty, George Augustus felt mightily insulted; Caroline demanded to witness the birth. 'At her labour', she declared, 'I positively will be.' But she wasn't. When Augusta's waters broke at a Kensington Palace soirée, her husband pushed her into a carriage and whisked her away. Afterwards, the prince received a blistering letter from his father:

> The professions you have lately made . . . of your particular
> regard to me, are so contradictory to all your actions that I
> cannot suffer myself to be imposed upon by them . . . This
> extravagant and undutiful behaviour, in so essential a point
> as the birth of an heir to my Crown, is such an evidence of
> your pre-meditated defiance . . . as cannot be excused by the
> pretended innocence of your intentions, nor palliated . . . by
> specious words only.[17]

The curse of the Guelphs was returning with a vengeance. Caroline's anguish preceded her painful death. She had been suffering for a while from an intestinal hernia, and needed a straightforward surgical operation. Some accounts state that gangrene set in unexpectedly, others that the surgery was botched. At all events, the queen-electress never recovered. Writhing in agony, she refused to see 'Fred'; George Augustus tried to sleep in a cot beside her. One of their last conversations touched on his life after her death. 'J'aurai des maîtresses,' he said. 'Cela n'empêche rien,' ('That's no obstacle,') she replied generously. Then she breathed her last.

The grief-stricken king-elector lived on for nearly a quarter of a century. Aged fifty-four, he still rode out with his troops, not letting his private troubles unnerve him. He repeatedly went to Hanover, where he refound a woman with whom he had earlier fathered a child. Amalie von Wallmoden (1704–65), a 'brunette with fine black eyes', divorced her husband, took the title of Countess of Yarmouth, and moved to London as the next *maîtresse-en-titre*. Permanently at the king-elector's side, she strengthened both the court's Germanic flavour and the whiff of corruption; she allegedly 'traded in bishoprics'. Her son, Johann Ludwig von Wallmoden-Gimborn (1736–1811), soldier, art collector and diplomat, was to become the electoral army's *Oberbefehlshaber* or officer commanding.[18]

Hanover revived the king-elector's spirits. To mark a visit in the summer of 1740 by his daughters, Anne and Mary, he organized a series of festivities that lasted for several days:

There were illuminations in the Herrenhaus Gardens and a masque in Hanover's opera house. [George Augustus] appeared in Turkish dress, accompanied by Sultana Wallmoden. Mary dressed up as a rural nymph. Anne added to the general mood of celebrations with her expert harpsichord playing and subtle singing.[19]

Even so, George Augustus cut off his wayward son; the two never spoke for five years, until meeting accidentally at a ball. The father said: 'How does the princess do?'; the son silently kissed his hand. Yet Frederick's marriage to Augusta flourished; they produced a large brood and a happy household, living either at Kew or at Cliveden in Buckinghamshire. Frederick became an active patron of the arts, a keen cricketer, and, like his father before him, the darling of the political opposition.

This time round, the split within the royal and electoral family ran deep, prompting the crystallization of two mutually antagonistic political groupings – one the pro-monarchical loyalists, the other the self-styled 'Patriots'. Robert Walpole steered a tortuous middle course between the Scylla of the 'pro-Hanoverians' and the Charybdis of the 'native Britons'.

The loyalists supported everything that flowed from the Hanoverian Succession. Their best representative was the 'eccentric genius' John Carteret, Earl Granville (1690–1763), Channel Islander, Virginian landowner, sometime ambassador to Sweden and Prussia and a popular Lord Lieutenant of Ireland. A fluent German-speaker, 'Three-bottle Carteret' became the king-elector's favourite but fell foul of Walpole, before later gaining the powerful post of President of the Privy Council. He was denounced by William Pitt, the protoplastic Brexiteer, as 'an execrable, a sole minister, who has renounced the British nation'.[20]

For their part, the Patriots were appalled both by Walpole's stranglehold on Parliament and by what they perceived as the king-elector's neglect of British interests. George Augustus appeared to them as a small-minded bigot who disliked everything English – as summarized by Lord Hervey:

> No English cook could dress a dinner, no English player could act, no English coachman could drive, no English jockey ride, nor were English horses fit to drive or be ridden; no Englishman knew how to come into a room, nor any Englishwoman how to dress herself, whereas at Hanover all these things were the utmost perfection.[21]

Whether or not this assessment was remotely fair is another matter. Much of the British public, and many peevish British biographers, have treated George Augustus's attachment to his German homeland as 'an obvious defect'. In the 1730s, parts of the English press coined the epithet of 'the King who wasn't there', after a mischievous placard was hung on his palace gates: 'Lost or strayed out of this house, a man who has left a wife and six children: whoever will give any tidings of him to the churchwardens of St James's parish ... shall receive four shillings and sixpence reward.'[22]

Yet the king-elector's 'Hanoverianism' cannot be reasonably equated with wilful neglect of Great Britain. The common cause which he sought to promote viewed the interests of Great Britain and of the Electorate as complementary, and the principal implication for foreign policy was that Great Britain should play its part in European affairs and avoid an insular, isolationist line.[23]

Originally, the polar opposite to loyalism had been Jacobitism. But the collapse of the 'Fifteen' heralded an alternative variant, which excoriated the Hanoverians without praising the Stuarts. Adopting the war cry of 'Liberty', these Patriots first coalesced round William Pulteney, Earl of Bath (1684–1764), an anti-Walpole Whig, and Henry St John, Viscount Bolingbroke (1678–1751), an ex-Jacobite Tory, publisher of *The Craftsman* (1726–35) and author of *The Idea of a Patriot King* (1738). Leading recruits included the brothers-in-law Lord Cobham of Stowe and the above-mentioned William Pitt, who was combining simultaneous careers as military officer and MP. Walpole dubbed them 'disturbers of the government', and terminated Pitt's commission. They launched the 'Opera of the Nobility' in Lincoln's Inn Fields to spite Handel's King's Theatre in the Haymarket. For a while, they even won over the young Samuel Johnson, who directed some pointed barbs at the monarch:

> Here let those reign, whom Pensions can incite
> To vote a Patriot black, and a Courtier white.
> Explain their Country's dear-bought Rights away
> And plead for pirates in the light of day.
> With slavish tenets taint our poison'd youth
> And lend a Lye the Confidence of Truth.[24]

Then, one day in August 1740 at Cliveden, in a masque attended by Prince Frederick, a patriotic song composed by Dr Thomas Arne was premiered:

When Britain first, at Heaven's command
Arose from out the azure main,
This was the charter of the land,
And guardian angels sang this strain:
Rule, Britannia! Britannia rule the waves.
Britons never will be slaves.[25]

Few who sing these words today realize that they make a sly allusion to the slave trade and point to George Augustus as the would-be slave master.

Fertility is one of the greatest dynastic virtues, and one whereby the Hanoverian Guelphs easily beat their Stuart rivals. George Augustus produced seven surviving children, his son Frederick nine, and his grandson George thirteen. William, Duke of Cumberland (1721–65) avoided matrimony, but three of his sisters – Anne in 1734, Mary in 1740 and Louise in 1743 – were married respectively to a Prince of Orange, a *Landgraf* of Hesse-Cassel, and a King of Denmark. Late in life, George Augustus approached the Duke of Brunswick-Wolfenbüttel to take a high-maintenance granddaughter off his hands.[26]

In contrast, the Jacobite challenge was scuppered by lack of heirs. James Edward Stuart (1688–1766), the Old Pretender, lived on in Roman exile. But his bachelor sons, Charles Edward Stuart, the Young Pretender (1720–88) and his cardinal brother, Henry, packed no credible dynastic promise.

So the dismal chorus of the Patriots gradually subsided. During the Austrian war, Pitt notoriously described Britain as 'a province of the execrable Protectorate'.[27] Yet, ironically, the Jacobite Rising of 1745 (see below) helped to heal political divisions. For all their faults, the 'Hanoverians' were preferable to the Stuarts. Courtiers began to attend both courts, and on 15 October 1745 the *Gentleman's Magazine* published 'a new song for two voices':

> God save great GEORGE, our King,
> Long live our noble King,
> God save our King.
> Send him victorious.
> Happy and glorious,
> Long to reign over us,
> God save our King.[28]

Wrongly called 'the National Anthem', the song was enthusiastically sung in London theatres, and, after Culloden, adopted at court, where a courtier remarked: 'I have never seen the [king-elector] in such glee.'

Familial tensions eased too. 'He was a more tender grandfather', Horace Walpole noted of the ageing monarch, 'than he had ever been a father.' He even sent his advice to Prince Frederick: 'God has given you so high a mark to govern one day, and if you don't please them, they won't please you in return. Please read this carefully . . . as it comes from a Father, who (what is not usual) is your best Friend.'[29]

George Augustus was trying hard. But final reconciliation evaded him. In March 1751 at Cliveden, Prince Frederick was hit in the chest by a cricket ball, developed pleurisy and expired. His father uttered: 'Il est mort.' The widow burned her husband's papers, leaving little beyond one immortal epitaph:

Here lies poor Fred
Who was alive and is dead . . .
There is no more to be said.[30]

Among his offspring, Fred left the future major-general, Charles Marsack (1736–1820); his eldest legitimate son, George, was the new heir apparent.

The king-elector now set out to mend family fences. In September 1756, he offered his eighteen-year-old heir a handsome birthday present of £40,000 to set up his own establishment. Prince George dared to decline: 'I hope that I shall not be thought wanting in the Duty which I owe your Majesty, if I humbly continue to entreat your Majesty's permission to remain with the Princess, my Mother. This point is of too great consequence to my happiness for me not to wish ardently your Majesty's favour & indulgence.'[31] Permission was granted. The family was returning to a more even keel.

Increasingly beset by wars and the threatened resurgence of Prince Frederick's Patriots, George Augustus soldiered stoically on. But he was no pushover. When his younger son, Cumberland, encountered difficulties commanding British forces in Germany, he tried to defend him against the backstabbers. 'Knowing your affection for me,' he wrote, 'I never shall impute to you the negligence of those old fools by whose stupidity you find yourself distressed.'[32] He held out against admitting William Pitt to his government until December 1756.

Biographers are obliged to balance their subjects' defects with their virtues. George Augustus may indeed have been 'a touchy, comic, and obstinate, small man'.[33] And his inter-personal skills undoubtedly lacked finesse. In one of Lady Mary Wortley Montagu's *bons mots*, 'He looked on all men and women as creatures he might kick or kiss for his diversion.' Yet that was not all. After thirty years on the throne, the inept little man was confounding his critics. He had shown resolve under adversity, had outlived or accommodated his opponents; had gripped the helm firmly or bent to the gale as necessary; and the ship of his family's composite state sailed on.

6

George Augustus:
A Political Animal

The political views of George Augustus are clouded in obscurity; he played his cards very close to his chest. But much may be gleaned from circumstance. Seeing his generally cautious attitude, one may safely assume that he was wedded to a conservative approach, stressing sound management, stability, security and self-preservation. All sources underline his punctiliousness and penny-pinching. 'Exactitude', wrote one biographer, 'was his passion.'[1]

The king-elector undoubtedly understood the difference between the continental divine right of kings and English ideas of limited monarchy. His German background would also have taught him – what few Britishers grasped – that Protestantism was no safeguard against absolutism; numerous Protestant princes, whom he knew, professed unmistakably absolutist ideals.[2] Privately, he could well have imagined that his anointed person embodied God-given sovereignty; Walpole once reported that 'he wishes to be absolute.' Yet, publicly, he guarded his tongue and kept everyone guessing. With the Stuarts out and the Guelphs in, no one was going to interrogate him. And, since no laws were openly flouted, he was left in peace.

George II Augustus, however, was juggling with two political systems, not one. He was not just King of Great Britain. '[His] perspective and outlook were European,' writes his latest biographer wisely, 'and he thought in terms of his domains and territories rather than about national boundaries.'[3] Even so, most historians continue to judge him exclusively by their ideas of unchanging English constitutionalism, and presume that he took a back seat in government, handing business to powerful British ministers. This picture is questionable. Numerous descriptions of his governing style show him at the centre of affairs, dealing methodically with everyone and everything.

Within the Electorate, the monarch acted as the patriarchal *Landesvater*, severe and merciful by turns. He followed his father's *Reglement* of 1714, which made provision for the German Chancery's migration to London and for the co-ordination of its activities with Hanover. In his absence, the electoral Privy Councillors were authorized to convene the Estates of the dependent territories, to instruct ambassadors, to react to military emergencies, to sign off policy decisions *ad mandatum nostrum* and to settle most petitions on site. At the same time, when selecting important issues for referral to London, they were instructed to present unanimous proposals. Their chairman, like his British counterpart, gradually acquired the title of premier minister. Under George Augustus, three such premiers held office: Count von Bothmer (to 1732), Heinrich, Baron Grote (1735–53) and Gerlach Adolph, Baron von Münchhausen (from 1753).[4]

Within the larger arena of the Holy Roman Empire, a

prince-elector was obliged above all to cultivate relations with successive emperors, his feudal masters, to whom he owed military service and from whom he sought reciprocal benefits. Securing confirmation of the enfeoffment of Bremen-Verden, for example, demanded years of pleading. During his reign, three emperors held sway in Vienna: the Habsburg Charles VI (r. 1711–40), the Wittelsbach Charles VII (r. 1742–5), and Maria Theresa's husband, Francis of Lorraine (r. 1745–65). Beyond that, George Augustus and his representatives engaged in the convoluted politics not only of the Perpetual Imperial Diet in Regensburg, but also of the College of Electors, the College of Princes (as Duke of Lauenberg), and the Assembly of Protestant Princes, the *Corpus Evangelicorum*. After the Saxon elector's conversion to Catholicism in 1697, they constantly opposed his continuing tenure of the *Corpus's* presidency.

In Great Britain, the king-elector faced another set of laws, practices and institutions. The main divide is conventionally described as that between the dual spheres of royal prerogative and parliamentary competence, frequently accompanied by an assumption of parliamentary supremacy. The reality was more ambiguous. Once former religious passions had subsided, the Westminster Parliament was content to give ground to the monarchical executive. In early Georgian times, the monarch acted as the central lynchpin of an aristocratic system, where the self-same people paid obeisance at court, filled the Lords, controlled the Commons and hogged the offices of state.

The career of Charles Watson-Wentworth, Marquess of Rockingham (1730–82), nicely illustrates the way government worked. Embarking on his grand tour aged twenty-one, Rockingham made a detour to Herrenhausen on the Duke of Newcastle's advice to meet the king-elector in person. He left with the post of Gentleman of the Bedchamber, getting a start which took him to vice-admiral, to Garter Knight in 1760, and twice thereafter to prime minister.[5]

A German prince may not have seen much difference between Whig lords and Tory grandees, except for the latters' Jacobite past. The king-elector naturally relied heavily on the Whigs, who, having led the opposition to the Stuarts, had now tied their colours to the Hanoverian mast. But he did not shun their Tory rivals completely. The Tory Viscounts Deerhurst, father and son, Earls of Coventry, of Croome Court, Worcestershire, held the lord-lieutenancy of their county in turn.

The key mechanism lay in judicious patronage. The king-elector held in his gift hundreds of high government, ecclesiastical and military appointments, and he required all post-holders both to swear an oath of allegiance and to abjure the Pretenders.[6] By putting a fair proportion of those posts at the disposal of his Whig ministers, not least of Walpole, he built up a self-perpetuating political machine which oversaw a decisive block of loyalists in government and Parliament for the duration.

As recently evolved, the British Cabinet was essentially a committee of the Privy Council. The First Lord of the Treasury, acting as chief minister, created the vital bridge between sovereign and Parliament. The Secretaries of State for the Southern and Northern Departments, and the Lord President of the Council were necessary members. The Southern

Secretary attended to southern England, Ireland, the colonies and the Catholic world: the Northern Secretary to northern England, Scotland and the Protestant states.

Chief ministers, *nota bene*, were appointed and dismissed entirely at the sovereign's will, functioning in an environment which, for their own preservation, encouraged them to disarm Parliament and to fix elections. Even Walpole, who held sway to 1742, could tremble when entering the king-elector's private chamber. George August might end a consultation with 'Do as you please!', but such consultations were regular and unavoidable. The practice continued after Walpole was briefly succeeded by Wilmington, and for ten years from 1744 by the 'Broad Bottom ministry' of Henry Pelham and Pelham's brother, the Duke of Newcastle, labelled 'the epitome of mediocrity'. Two short-lived 'Silly ministries', which never obtained the seals of office, entered the record – one in 1746, another a decade later. The Duke of Devonshire officiated in 1756–7, before Newcastle returned. William Pitt dominated the later wartime Cabinets without becoming prime minister until the following reign.

Managing the ministers presented a major challenge to George Augustus. Horace Walpole states that he could be 'imposed upon' by clever politicians. 'Queen Caroline governed him by dissimulation ... Robert Walpole by his ... influence in Parliament, Granville by flattery ... and the Duke of Newcastle by teasing and betraying him.'[7] Yet the sovereign always took the decisions. 'I am come to direct you,' joked the Duke of Grafton on receiving an audience, 'who shall be your minister.'[8]

Those relationships could prove emotional. When Walpole fell to his knees to kiss hands for the final farewell, George Augustus burst helplessly into tears;[9] despite Walpole's weariness and fading influence in Parliament, the king-elector had begged him to stay on. After appointing Newcastle, he exploded with disgust, bemoaning the circumstances which compelled him 'to take [a man], who is not fit to be chamberlain in Germany's smallest court'.[10] Politicians who raised suspicions of disloyalty, like the Earl of Berkeley, could be brutally banished.[11]

Nonetheless, George Augustus willingly sought advice. In 1751, when hesitating over the Duke of Cumberland's suitability to be regent-elect, he pressed Henry Fox, Baron Holland (1705–74) – the father of Charles James Fox – for a straight opinion:

King-elector:	What do you say against the bill? Tell me honestly, do you like it?
Henry Fox:	If you ask me, Sir – No.
King-elector:	I thank you for that. My affection is with my son . . . I don't know why they dislike him . . .

In the end, the monarch conceded; Princess Augusta was appointed under a Regency Council.[12]

The king-elector's alleged anti-British bias caused recurring trouble. Pitt's 'Patriot Boys' constantly complained, and Horace Walpole suggested that the monarch could indeed be unreasonable. 'May the devil take your bishops and . . . your ministers,' George Augustus was once reported as saying, '[take] ... your Parliament ... and your whole island, provided I can get out of it and go to Hanover.' Yet it takes two to tangle, and the complainers themselves were far from innocent. Should the king-elector take all the blame? For the Patriots' language was invariably condescending – 'England has conferred vast benefits on you' – or, referring to the Electorate as 'a foreign and unimportant principality', downright insulting. If a German had dared to say the same about England, the Patriots would have been furious. And they didn't stop at insults. Legal advice was sought in the hope of forcing the monarch to renounce his continental titles and possessions.[13]

Furthermore, additional offence could have been caused by George Augustus's willingness to play the role of Imperial vassal too assiduously. The Patriots no doubt disliked it intensely; but the established principle in those days, as stated by Chamberlayne, was that the British monarch 'acknowledges Precedence only to the Emperor'.[14]

The king-elector's British ministers competed for time and access with his electoral ministers, who used a suite of offices in St James's Palace immediately adjacent to his own. The German Chancery's staff of selected electoral Privy Councillors was headed at first by Count von Bothmer, the Electorate's premier, who was succeeded in the Chancery by Johann Philipp von Hattorf in 1732–7, by Ernst von Steinberg in 1737–48, and by Philipp Adolph von Münchhausen from 1748. A swarm of clerks, chefs, physicians and pastors attended. Their general secretary, Gerhard Andreas Reiche, presided for forty-four years to 1758, working daily alongside George Augustus. Theoretically, all Chancery operations were financed from the Electorate's *Englische Kasse*, but in practice, contrary to British rules, frequently from the king-elector's Privy Purse.[15]

The monarch's German business depended on a regular flow of correspondence with Hanover, and hence on an elaborate postal network. To facilitate matters, George Augustus bought out the private managers of the Electorate's Post Office in 1735. Postal stations and stables dotted the route to the Dutch coast, supporting a rota of express couriers and monthly heavy transports. Sensitive correspondence was encrypted, and electoral censors operated 'black chambers' at the interception posts of Nienburg and Wildhausen. The highly skilled Hanoverian intelligence service was said to share its expertise with British counterparts.[16] Parliament often protested the expense of the two secret services, on both of which the king-elector could call. The office of Keeper of the Privy Purse, who paid and supervised the secret services, was held for thirty years by Baron Augustus Schutz (1689–1757), an electoral diplomat's son, who owned Shotover Park near Oxford. The expert cryptographer/codebreaker most frequently used in Britain was Bishop Edward Willes (1693–1773), Dean of London and Bishop of Bath and Wells, who was rewarded with regular ecclesiastical advancements. Willes had made his name in the 1720s, deciphering the correspondence of the convicted Jacobite Bishop Atterbury, and later set up a family business with his son.[17]

In the British system, the relationship between king-elector and Parliament was central, and in this period both sides avoided trials of strength. Government managers hovered over both the elevation of peers and the make-up of the Commons. Long-serving ministers, such as Walpole or Newcastle, bridged the gap between monarch and parliamentarians, and the impact of Crown placemen and pensioners among MPs ensured that government funds were never denied. Political culture was manifestly corrupt, and parliamentary language tediously obsequious. On 16 February 1738 Old Style, for example (27 February 1739 New Style), the House of Lords was thanking the king-elector for opening Great Britain's eighth Parliament:

> Most gracious Sovereign, We, your Majesty's most dutiful and loyal Subjects, the Lords Spiritual and Temporal ... beg leave to [offer] our humble thanks for your most gracious speech ... The Honour of your Majesty's Crown and the interest of your People are ... inseparable, and, as your Majesty hath on all Occasions demonstrated to the World, you have both equally at Heart ... The gracious Regard, which your Majesty is pleased to express for the Resolutions and Advice of your Parliament, is a great instance of your royal Goodness ...[18]

One imagines George Augustus, baffled by the verbiage, longing for the conclusion, as if waiting for the verb at the end of a prolix German sentence. Occasionally, proceedings could be raucous. In 1728, Kitty Douglas, Duchess of Queensberry, repeatedly took a bevy of noisy peeresses to the Lords' gallery demanding the release of John Gay, the poet and dramatist, who was well known to the monarch, having served in Hanover as a diplomat, and who was briefly detained for his persistent mockery of Walpole.

The king-elector's dealings with the Commons followed a well-worn pattern. Traditionally, he only entered the Commons' Chamber during the opening session to outline his financial demands: 'Gentlemen of the Commons! I have ordered Estimates to be set before you for the service of the ensuing year, and I must desire you to grant such supplies as the circumstances of affairs require . . .'[19]

A furious debate would then erupt. Opposition MPs, such as the fiery Jacobite William Shippen, would denounce the billowing costs of the national debt. Crown ministers would beg to differ, and at the closing vote would always 'have the numbers'. Thanks to careful management by Walpole and Newcastle, the king-elector's government controlled the Commons and not vice versa. 'The power of ministerial influence was now so great,' Tories lamented, 'that nothing could check it.'[20]

At the start of the reign, George Augustus had not enjoyed such a comfortable position. In 1733, he and his chief minister, Walpole, were forced to withdraw an Excise Bill owing to mounting opposition in the Commons. Only after that humiliation did they put measures in place to prevent a repetition.

The king-elector stood aloof from the general elections, held in 1727, 1734, 1741, 1747 and 1754. In 'the golden age of the rotten boroughs' voting was often uproarious and shamelessly rigged.[21] Peers of the realm typically dominated their counties and shoed their hand-picked parliamentary candidates into their seats, before using their 'squadrons' of clients and placemen to pass their desired legislation.

After the abortive Jacobite Rising of 1745, when George Augustus could project a more assertive political image, his chosen medium was opera. Filled with soaring music, Handel's production of *Solomon* (1749) employed unabashed absolutist imagery worthy of Versailles:

> From East to West
> Who so wise as Solomon?
> Who like Israel's king is blessed,
> Who so worthy of a throne?[22]

Whenever the king-elector left London for Hanover – on average every other year – the so-called 'English Chancery', a Cabinet sub-committee headed by a secretary of state, joined his entourage. The arrangement worked well except in 1736, when prolonged stormy weather stranded George Augustus and his party at Helvetsluys in Holland over Christmas. The *London Gazette* kept meticulous track of his movements, always commenting on his good health:

> Helvetsluys, December 21 NS. The King left Hanover about Ten of the Clock on Tuesday night the 18th instant ... and came to this place [today] a little after Seven in the evening, where he continues in perfect health.
>
> December 25 NS. His Britannick Majesty arrived at Helvetsluys in good health on Friday last ... His Majesty is detained there by contrary winds.
>
> December 25–28. His Majesty, having sailed from Helvoetsluys for England about 11 in the morning, and having been Thirty Hours at sea in very boisterous weather ... was obliged to return again to that Harbour ...

11–15th January 1736. On the 13th inst, the King embarked on board the Carolina yacht at Helvetsluys, the wind being SW by W . . . [and] landed in good health at Loestoff in Suffolk yesterday at Noon. That night His Majesty lay at Stratford in the same county, [afterwards] passing in an open chaise through the City of London [and arriving] at St James's at Two in the afternoon (God be praised).[23]

On another occasion, a Dutch innkeeper charged him £100 for a round of drinks. 'Are coffee and gin so terribly scarce round here?' asked an aide. 'No,' the innkeeper replied, 'but Kings are!'[24]

Sovereign monarchs ruling by hereditary right scorned popularity ratings. But a Georgian psephologist would have easily spotted marked peaks and troughs in the king-elector's record. Apparently, he was always extremely popular in the American colonies.[25] In Britain, as Prince of Wales with Caroline at his side, he outshone his father; thanks to the Patriots' onslaught up to 1745, his reputation slipped. After Culloden, he never looked back.

All in all, the array of political games which the king-elector played was formidable, and, in a stewardship of over three decades, it was no mean achievement to keep his footing. Furthermore, one must recognize steady improvement in the monarch's performance. In the 1730s, in Walpole's time, his personal impact was modest. In the 1740s, he overcame attempts to topple him both in Germany and in Britain. In the 1750s, he was unchallengeable. He learned the monarchical trade slowly, but was nearer to mastery of it at the end than at the beginning.

7

On the Throne, Part II – Poets, Pardons and Prerogatives

Though the reign of George Augustus formed an unbroken continuum of thirty-three years and passed through several distinct phases, most of his trickiest moments occurred in the earlier part. By the time that he faced the Jacobite Rising in 1745–6, he had only just reached the halfway mark. Moving into the third decade, he was mightily reassured by the Rising's failure. As a military man, he accepted the fortunes of battle with stoicism and soldiered on, perhaps with less energy but definitely with more confidence.

CULTURE

'I hate all boets and bainters' is a none-too-clever misquotation carried by almost all the websites relating to George Augustus.[1] It is improbable that he mangled his words in that way; 'p' is *not* an English consonant normally mispronounced by German-speakers. Elsewhere, George Augustus asked: 'Who is this Pope? Why can't my subjects write in prose?'[2] The quotation, which sounds like a joke that misfired, is another godsend for those wishing to dismiss George Augustus as a boorish philistine. Yet, even if accurate, these outbursts hardly convey the full picture. True, the monarch enjoyed deer-hunting, card games and military dress, and avoided competing with his wife, Caroline. Even so, he was also an avid theatregoer and opera buff, and a generous patron of music and learning.

In this last respect, the king-elector consistently supported Georg Friedrich Händel, a Saxon immigrant, who outshone all his English contemporaries,[3] composing forty-two operas, twenty-nine oratorios and 120 cantatas, and giving the reign a brilliant accompaniment. The *Water Music* suites or 'Handel's Largo' – the aria '*Ombra mai fù*' from the opera *Serse* (1738) – were but sublime moments in decades of delight. During the *Messiah's* first London performance in 1743, George Augustus reputedly saluted the 'Hallelujah Chorus' by standing to his feet.[4] The grand *Music for the Royal Fireworks* (1749) greeted peace. Handel's mastery of melody rarely slipped:

> Where'er you walk
> Cool gales shall fan the glade
> Trees where you sit
> Shall crowd into a shade
>
> Where'er you tread
> The blushing flowers shall rise
> And all things flourish
> Where'er you turn your eyes[5]

Exactly to his patron's taste, Händel embodied the perfect fusion of German and British elements, in the process becoming Handel.

And there were others to be admired. John Stanley (1712–86), the blind organist of the Inner Temple's chapel, whose 'Trumpet Voluntary' is a Baroque showpiece, would have known that the great Handel was frequently in his audience.[6]

The king-elector's household permanently employed a Poet Laureate and a Master of the King's Musick, requiring them to produce musical odes for the New Year and the monarch's birthday. Over the years, George Augustus listened to over sixty such compositions by successive music masters: John Eccles (to 1735), Maurice Greene (1735–55) and the talented William Boyce (from 1755).[7]

The Poet Laureateship caused huge controversy. In 1730, George Augustus handed the post to the Danish-born actor-manager of Drury Lane Theatre, Colley Cibber. Variously described as 'brash', 'shady' and 'tasteless', Cibber played the star roles of Restoration Comedy. His racy memoir, *An Apology ...* (1740) aroused many sniggers,[8] and he later starred in anthologies of bad verse:

> O say what is that thing call'd Light,
> Which I must ne'er enjoy;
> What are the blessings of the sight,
> O tell your poor blind boy![9]

George Augustus's fondness for Cibber-style comedy certainly signalled a need for light relief. Alexander Pope reacted otherwise. His satirical *Dunciad* (1734) portrayed Cibber as the 'King of Dunces', firing a feud which plumbed the depths of insult and indecency.[10]

The king-elector, another butt of satire, ignored it,

interesting himself instead in learning and higher education. In his capacity as *Summus Episcopus*, he loyally supported the great University of Göttingen, which he founded in 1734 and which, as the 'Georgia Augusta', was named after him; his lavish reception there in 1748 marked a highlight of many visits to Germany.[11] Two years earlier, he launched Princeton in New Jersey,[12] and in 1754 King's College, New York (now Columbia),[13] the parent college of the University of Halifax, Nova Scotia.[14] In the pre-modern age, few monarchs had the distinction of founding three famous universities. In 1753, he presented his library to the British Museum.[15] He is unlikely to have known much of the Scottish Enlightenment, whose renown matured only slowly, but would certainly have heard of the Scottish philosopher David Hume (1711–76), who first gained fame as the author of a best-selling *History of England*, which began to appear from 1754. (Hume's groundbreaking *A Treatise of Human Nature* (1739) had not been well received, falling, as he said, 'dead-born from the press'.)[16]

George Augustus was ex-officio patron of London's Royal Society, the world's first scientific association. For purely formal reasons, he was elected a Royal Fellow in July 1727, as was his son, Frederick. Three years later, undoubtedly at his initiative, two leading Habsburg courtiers, Francis, Duke of Lorraine, the future Emperor, and Count Philip Kinsky, were elected Fellows.[17] In 1751, he founded the Royal Society of Antiquaries.[18]

In that same year, the king-elector helped reform the calendar in the same scientific spirit. By clinging to the Julian calendar, England had lagged behind many of its neighbours,

University Foundations: 1734, Georgia Augusta University, Göttingen, (*top*); 1746, College of New Jersey, now Princeton, (*left*); 1754, King's College, New York, now Columbia, (*right*).

but the Calendar (New Style) Act of 1750 brought England into line in two ways. To many people's amazement, Tuesday 31 December 1751 was followed by Wednesday 1 January 1752, making 1751 a nine-month year (previously, the New Year had begun on Lady Day, 25 March). And then, in due course, Wednesday 2 September 1752 was followed by Thursday 14 September. Riots were reported, as England finally caught up with Scotland and Brunswick-Lüneburg.

1. Accession portrait, 1727. King-elector George II Augustus, otherwise 'George II', sovereign of a 'composite state' of two kingdoms, one Imperial Electorate and their dependencies.

2. The royal and electoral coat of arms of the Hanoverian Guelphs from 1714: (*top left*) Scotland, England, (*top right*) France, (*bottom left*) Ireland, (*bottom right*) Brunswick, Lüneburg, Westphalia and the Holy Roman Empire.

3. Riverside old Hanover, where George Augustus was born in the Leineschloss, largely destroyed by fire in 1741: showing (*centre*) the medieval Nuns' Tower and (*inset*) the rebuilt classical façade at the rear, which George Augustus would have known in his later years.

4. Georg August von Welf (*centre*), aged seven, *c.*1690, with his sister and his mother, Sophia Dorothea of Celle, who was soon to be incarcerated for life.

5. Caroline of Brandenburg-Ansbach by Sir Godfrey Kneller, 1716: George Augustus's wife from 1705, Princess of Wales from 1714, queen-electress from 1727.

. George Augustus's grandmother, Dowager Duchess Sophie of Brunswick-
Lüneburg-Calenberg, receiving news in 1701 of England's Act of Settlement,
which made her heiress to the Stuart line. James I looks down on the scene.

. King-elector George I Louis (*seated*), with George Augustus (*right*) in armour
as Prince of Wales; no love was lost between them. Detail from a painting by
James Thornhill, Upper Hall, Greenwich, *c*.1725.

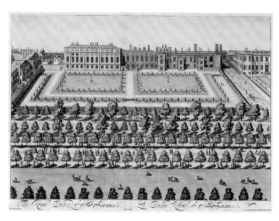

8. St James's Palace, London, 1730, the principal residence of early Georgian monarchs, seat of the Electorate's government in the German Chancery and of the royal and electoral Court of St James's.

9 & 10. George Augustus's alternative residences in Hanover and London

11. George II Augustus landing off Margate, watercolour by Peter Monamy, 1730. In peacetime the king-elector spent every other summer in Hanover, sailing between England and Holland.

12–16. (*Top left*) Great Britain, one crown, silver, 1746; obverse, the monarch's Roman-style armoured bust and laurel wreath, GEORGIUS II DEI GRATIA (George II, Thanks be to God). (*Top right*) Ireland, regal copper halfpenny, 1746; reverse, Irish harp with crown, HIBERNIA. (*Centre*) Great Britain, two guineas, gold, 1738; reverse, royal and electoral coat of arms, B ET L DUX SRI IAT ET E MB FR ET H REX FT (Brunswick and Lüneburg Duke, Holy Roman Empire Arch-treasurer and Elector, Great Britain, France and Ireland King, Defender of the Faith). (*Bottom left*) Brunswick-Lüneburg, 1/6 *Thaler*, silver, 1731; reverse, Westphalian horse, NEC ASPERA TERRENT (Lest Difficulties Cause Fear). (*Bottom right*) Brunswick-Lüneburg, one *Thaler*, silver, 1757, reverse, *Wildermann* with club (a folkloric figure of the Harz Mountains), BR ET LUN DUX SRI ATH ET EL (Brunswick and Lüneburg Duke, Holy Roman Empire Arch-treasurer and Elector).

17. Johann Kaspar von Bothmer (1656–1732) occupied 'The House at Cockpit Corner' (Downing Street) from 1716 to 1732 and headed the German Chancery in London.

18. Sir Robert Walpole (1676–1745), Britain's first prime minister, occupied 'Downing Street' from 1735, resigning in 1742. *Quieta non movere.*

19. Thomas Pelham-Holles (1693–1768), Duke of Newcastle upon Tyne and Newcastle-under-Lyme, long-term Whig Party manager.

20. Gerlach Adolph, Freiherr von Münchhausen (1688–1770), relative of the world-famous fantasist, Baron von Münchhausen.

21. Henrietta Howard (1689–1767), née Hobart, Countess of Suffolk. George Augustus's first mistress – 'a reasonable woman, handsome and witty, yet a friend' (Pope).

22. Amalie von Wallmoden (1704–65), née von Wendt, Countess of Yarmouth, vendor of bishoprics and George Augustus's principal mistress from the mid 1730s until his death.

23. James Edward Stuart (1688–1766), the 'Old Pretender', self-styled King James III, father of 'Bonnie Prince Charlie'; George Augustus's rival.

24. King-elector August III of Saxony-Poland (1696–1763), aka Friedrich August II, George Augustus's neighbour in Germany.

25. Not all the king-elector's battles were victorious. At Fontenoy (1745), the French army's Irish Brigade (*left*) helped defeat the multinational Pragmatic Army. All the soldiers shown here were the king-elector's subjects.

26. HMS *Royal George*, the largest warship in the world (*right*), painted in 1757 in a semi-fictitious dockyard scene. In that decade, the Royal Navy began to rule the world's waves, as declared in the song 'Rule, Britannia', composed in 1740.

George II Augustus may not have commissioned many fine buildings, but his entourage contained numerous wealthy courtiers passionate about architecture, notably Richard Boyle, Lord Burlington (1694–1753), the 'Apollo of the Arts'. Many magnificent country houses, such as Chatsworth, Blenheim or Castle Howard, were adorned by Lancelot 'Capability' Brown (1716–83), landscape artist extraordinary, who refashioned hundreds of English parks.[19] By extending Stowe House and its gardens, Earl Temple made them into the finest example of Palladianism in the land.[20]

In painting, court patronage promoted the careers of both Joshua Reynolds (1723–92) and Thomas Gainsborough (1727–88). The Swiss portraitist Jean-Étienne Liotard (1702–89) worked in London in 1753–4. Yet the star was William Hogarth (1697–1764), whose moralistic sequential art, as in *The Rake's Progress* (1735) or *Gin Lane* (1751), shamed the courtiers' lifestyle.[21]

The aloof and rigid Hanoverian regime, which George Augustus inherited, invited satire. Jonathan Swift, Henry Carey, Alexander Pope and John Gay egged each other on. The 'whiplash pen' of the Anglo-Irish cleric 'Dean' Swift (1667–1745) produced *Gulliver's Travels* (1726) on the eve of the reign and *A Modest Proposal* (1729), purportedly advocating infant cannibalism, soon afterwards. Henry Carey celebrated the king-elector in a spoof eulogy:

> Smile, smile,
> Blest Isle.
> Grief past
> At last . . .

NEW KING,

BELLS RING.

NEW QUEEN,

BLEST SCENE.

Britain

Again

Revives

And thrives ...

Fear flies,

Stocks rise,

Wealth flows,

Art grows ...

Those out

May pout.

Those in

Will grin.

Great, small,

Pleased all.

God send

No end

To line

Divine

Of George and Caroline.[22]

Both George Augustus and Robert Walpole found themselves in the crosshairs of John Gay (1685–1732), once secretary to the British ambassador to Hanover. Gay's *Beggar's Opera* (1728), a rollicking tale of highwaymen, burglars, 'Trulls' and 'Doxies', was reputedly 'the most popular play of the century'. Pope wrote Gay's epitaph:

> Life is a jest, and all things show it.
> I thought it once, but now I know it.[23]

Pope – translator of Homer and Virgil, effortless fashioner of heroic couplets, and philosophical author of major works like the *Essay on Man* (1733–4) – never spared the king-elector's blushes:

> For sure, if Dulness sees a grateful Day,
> 'Tis in the shade of arbitrary Sway . . .
> May you, my Cam and Isis, teach it long!
> The RIGHT DIVINE OF KINGS to govern wrong.[24]

After the early 1740s, however, the snipers retreated, and George Augustus weathered the cultural storms. Samuel Johnson, for one, lost patience with the 'patriotic' political satire. 'Patriotism', Johnson wrote to Lord Chesterfield, 'is the last refuge of a scoundrel.'[25] In his milestone *Dictionary of the English Language* (1755), he listed ELECTOR as: '2. A prince who has a voice in the choice of the German emperour'; EMPEROUR as 'A monarch of title and dignity superior to a king', and KING as: 'Monarch, supreme governour'.[26] The dedicatee would definitely have approved.

Under George Augustus, however, no other literary figures matched the success of the novelists – Samuel Richardson (1689–1761), Henry Fielding (1707–54) and Fielding's sister, Sarah (1710–68). Richardson, a London printer, gained instant fame with his epistolary novel, *Pamela; or, Virtue Rewarded* (1740).[27] Sarah Fielding wrote a pioneering children's book, *The Governess* (1744)[28] and Henry Fielding, a Patriot friend of Pitt, launched a new comic genre with *Tom*

Jones (1749).[29] Richardson produced an unending stream of memorable one-liners: 'Marriage is the highest state of friendship', 'Love is not a volunteer thing', 'Familiarity destroys reverence', and 'Calamity is the test of integrity.' Henry Fielding, a magistrate, who founded the Bow Street Runners,[30] also penned the era's most rousing lyrics:

> When mighty roast beef was the Englishman's food
> It ennobled our hearts and enriched our blood.
> Our soldiers were brave and our courtiers were good.
> Oh, for the roast beef of old England,
> And 'Here's to old England's roast beef'.[31]

LAW

George Augustus had much to do with law and law-making, which were naturally major conversational topics among his aristocratic and courtly entourage. He made law by decree in Germany, and dealt in the British Isles with three jurisdictions and two legislative assemblies; his position, according to Chamberlayne, was '*Summus Totius Justicarius*, the Supreme Judge ... the Fountain from whence all Justice is derived'.[32] England's Common Law differed from both French-based Scottish Law and Irish Law. Since 1707, the Westminster Parliament had enacted British statute law, with the House of Lords being the highest court of appeal. The ancient Poynings' Law subjected all Irish legislation to English approval. Ironically, it was a German monarch who made English the obligatory language in all the courts of 'that part of Great Britain called England'.[33] Before 1730, all court records had been kept in Latin, and the court-rooms were filled with a cacophony of English, Latin and Law French.

By then, the emphasis of British statute law had moved from the constitutional and ecclesiastical sectors to commerce, crime and property. Under George II Augustus, roughly half of parliamentary acts addressed private purposes, especially toll roads and enclosures. The so-called 'Bloody Code' attached the death penalty to three times the previous number of offences.[34] Deterrence was the watchword. As the Marquess of Halifax said: 'Men are not hanged for stealing horses but that horses may not be stolen.' The Murder Act of 1751 (25 Geo II c 7) declared 'that all persons found guilty of wilful murder be executed on the day but one of the sentence passed'.[35] Many convicts were spared the ultimate penalty, then branded or deported to the colonies. Dr Johnson's aphorism 'Hanging wonderfully concentrates the mind' matched the spirit of the age.[36]

The law was seen as the guardian of morals and propriety. In 1736, the ancient body of witchcraft law was repealed; in 1750 a draconian Act to Prevent the Stealing of Turnips was passed, and in 1751 the Disorderly Houses Act to curb prostitution. Over the years, dozens of bills on lewdness, adultery, oaths and profanity crossed the king-elector's desk: 'By statute of George II ... every labourer, sailor or soldier swearing profanely shall forfeit one shilling ... and every other person under the degree of a gentleman two shillings, and every gentleman or person of rank five shillings ... and on the second offence double ...'.[37]

The Gin Acts of 1736 and 1751 raised much revenue

while aiming to control alcohol consumption. In total, 1,422 acts were passed during the reign, an average of forty-three per annum. In one sample year, 1746 (20 Geo II), fifty-two acts reached the statute book:

Aliens Act 1746, c 44

Berkshire Roads Act, 1746, c 6

Bruntisland Beer Duties Act 1746, c 26

Continuance of Acts 1746, c 47

Crown Lands, Forfeited Estates Act 1746, c 41

Distemper Among Cattle Act 1746, c 4

Distillers Act 1746, c 39

Dundee Beer Duties Act 1746, c 17

...

Traitors Transported Act 1746, c 46

Treason Act 1746, c 30

University of St Andrews Act 1746, c 32

Wales and Berwick Act 1746, c 32

Walton-Shepperton Bridge (Building and Tolls)
    Act 1746, c 22

Warrington to Wigan Road Act 1746, c 42

Wednesfield Chapel Act 1746, c 27

Will of Sir Joseph Jekyll Act 1746, c 34

Yarmouth Haven Act 1746, c 40.[38]

Every single Act required the monarch's assent, which he gave by attaching his Great Seal, but which he was entitled to refuse 'without rendering any Reason'.[39] Unlike his successors, the king-elector adorned his seal with all his titles: GEORGIUS II AUGUSTUS DEI GRATIA MAGNAE BRIT-ANNIAE FRANCIAE ET HIBERNIAE REX FIDEI DEFENSOR/

BRUNSWICKENSIS ET LUNEBURGENSIS DUX SACRI ROMANI
IMPERII ARCHITHESAURUS ET PRINCEPS ELECTOR.[40]

The personal involvement of George II Augustus in legal
matters, therefore, was paramount. He opened and closed
parliamentary sessions, appointed judges and granted
royal pardons. Though claiming to be merciful, he usually
dismissed petitions for pardon. One man pardoned, in
1727, was the Irish-American pirate John Vidal. Less for-
tunate was Paul Wells, an Oxford student, executed in
1749 for a minimal act of forgery.[41]

During the reign, several jurists rose to prominence. At
Göttingen, Professor Johann Pütter (1725–1807), was the
acknowledged master of the *ius publicum*.[42] In England,
George Augustus gave an earldom to his Lord Chancellor,
Philip Yorke, Lord Hardwicke (1690–1764) for greatly
expanding the law of equity,[43] and a barony to William Murray, Lord Mansfield (1705–93), a leading legal reformer.[44]
Both men made key rulings on slavery – one in support, the
other in opposition.[45] Sir William Blackstone (1723–80), an
Oxford professor, gained celebrity as a legal theorist, his
Analysis of the Laws of England (1756) and *Commentaries*
(1765) becoming classics.[46] Blackstone's Ratio stated: 'It is
better that ten guilty persons escape than that one innocent
be executed.'

Almost unnoticed, George Augustus was personally
acquainted with the greatest legal mind of his day. Charles-
Louis de Secondat, Baron de Montesquieu (1689–1755)
lived in London from 1729 to 1731, met Queen Caroline,
observed Parliament, read the English press and was duly
impressed by the extent of free speech. On his later travels

he dined with the king-elector at Herrenhausen, noting that his host was 'a great conversationalist'. Montesquieu's theory on the 'separation of powers' must surely have aroused the king-elector's interest. His *Esprit des Lois* (1748) contained numerous positive references to George Augustus's realms. 'England', he wrote, 'is the freest country in the world.'[47] Elsewhere it was reported that 'the only German state of which [Montesquieu] appeared to approve was Hanover.'[48] George Augustus can only have been delighted.

ARMED SERVICES

George Augustus was engaged with the military all his life. From 1727, however, he was hereditary commander-in-chief of the combined royal and electoral forces consisting of two armies and one navy, holding supreme prerogative powers. He and his top staff undoubtedly thought of those forces – as many British people did not – as a single, complex entity. To his mind, it was normal if electoral troops were deployed in Britain or America and British troops in Germany.

The unified electoral army, in which George Augustus once served, had started life in 1705, when the duchies of Calenberg and Celle merged their forces and fixed the regimental numbering. It consisted of thirty-two cavalry squadrons and twenty infantry battalions, making a standing army of around 30,000 men stationed at Hamelin, Hanover, Celle and Lüneburg.[49]

The electoral officer corps drew on noble-born professionals, often with experience in the Dutch, Prussian,

Hessian or Wolfenbüttel service. George Augustus was their *Oberbefehlshaber*. Other commanders included his son, *Reichsgraf* von Wallmoden-Gimborn, and Field-Marshal Friedrich von Spörcken.[50]

As the king-elector learned, the Royal Navy, Britain's 'wooden wall' and its senior service, had overwhelmingly English origins. Since the Restoration, in the era of Samuel Pepys, it had gradually established itself as a world-class force capable of founding a worldwide empire. In 1727 it possessed ninety-five capital ships of the line, divided into six classes, from first-raters of 100 guns to sixth-raters of twenty to twenty-eight guns, plus hundreds of lesser vessels.[51] The monarch, lacking naval experience, appointed the admirals, but habitually left them well alone.

In the eighteenth century naval technology changed slowly, and the great men-of-war stayed in service for decades. The navy's oldest first-rater, HMS *Royal William*, formerly the *Prince*, had been laid down in 1670 as the Duke of York's flagship, and stayed afloat until 1813. The upkeep of such ships demanded a rolling programme of refitting, a far-flung network of dockyards from Woolwich and Deptford to Antigua and Minorca, and a prodigious financial outlay.[52]

As George Augustus would discover, the navy's top flag officers followed promotion paths through four hierarchical squadrons – the Red, the White, the Yellow and the Blue. The highest officer, the admiral of the fleet, headed some twenty-five colleagues listed from admiral of the Red to rear-admiral of the Blue. To reach the top, ambitious officers needed to win an early commission in the captains' list. The most famous seadog of the age, Admiral Lord George Anson, circumnavigator of the world, served for fifty-one years, initially as a captain on the Carolina station, and eventually as a peer of the realm.[53]

The Board of the Admiralty, the navy's administrative department, was entrusted to the First Sea Lord. Anson held the post from 1751 to 1758, tightening discipline, improving medical care, reorganizing the fleets and re-establishing the Royal Marines. The king-elector was alive to the hardships of the service. Accidentally meeting a leg-less veteran, a captain of Marines, he awarded him half-pay for life on the spot.[54]

The British army, founded in 1707 through the merger of English and Scottish regiments, was always junior to the navy. Not much larger than its electoral partner, it was not in the top league of major continental formations. None-theless, as a trained cavalryman, the king-elector was happiest when reviewing his soldiers on the purpose-built Horse Guards Parade. The ceremony of Trooping the Col-our was instituted in 1748 to mark his birthday. The famous 'March from Scipio' was composed by Handel for the 1st of Foot.[55]

The British army's organization was a subject close to the monarch's heart; and the reign opened with the publication of a *Treatise of Military Discipline*.[56] The cavalry and inf-antry served alongside the Royal Artillery,[57] and a distinction was made between elite Household units and regular reg-iments of the line.[58] The Household establishment consisted of three regiments of horse – the Life Guards, Horse Gren-adiers and Royal Horse Guards (the Blues) – and three regiments of foot – the Coldstreams, Scots and Grenadiers, whose song was first printed in 1750:

> Some talk of Alexander and some of Hercules,
> Of Hector and Lysander, and of such great names as these.
> But of all the world's great heroes,
> There's none that ca-an compa-are,
> With a tow row, tow row, row, row, row,
> With the British Grenadiers.[59]

The regular cavalry consisted of seven regiments of heavy horse, starting with the 1st (King's) Dragoon Guards, and seventeen 'light' regiments of lancers; the infantry had seventy-one regiments. From 1751, all were numbered by seniority. The Royal Scots, founded in 1633, became the 1st Royal Regiment of Foot. Queen Caroline's 2nd Queen's Own Regiment had started out in 1714 as the Princess of Wales's Regiment.[60]

The king-elector attended his first parade on Blackheath near London after his coronation in October 1727, accompanied by the six-year old Duke of Cumberland. He continued to appear at parades, manoeuvres and, famously, on the battlefield for twenty years. After 1744 he was assisted by various chief commanders, including Field Marshals George Wade and Earl Ligonier.

Yet no British officer was more successful than John Manners, Marquess of Granby (1721–70), sometime Colonel of the Blues. Commissioned in 1745, George Augustus raised him in 1759 to be chief commander. Apart from his fine performance fighting the French at Minden, he is best remembered for setting up his veterans in business as publicans. In consequence, 'The Marquis of Granby' became one of the most popular names for English pubs.[61]

Aiming for quality rather than quantity, the royal and electoral land armies invariably fought in wartime within an Allied coalition. Such was the case both with the Pragmatic Army of 1742–8 and with the Army of Observation of 1757–8. It was a pattern very familiar to George Augustus, who had ridden into battle under Marlborough at Oudenarde.[62]

DIPLOMACY

Like military affairs, diplomacy lay within the monarch's jealously guarded prerogative, and the complicated business of sending one's own envoys abroad was complementary to the reception of foreign envoys (see Chapter 4). The sovereign alone nominated ambassadors and decided whither they were sent. So historians should be precise. Nowadays, British ambassadors serve in Vienna and Austrian ambassadors in London. Under the king-elector the Plenipotentiary Envoy of His Britannic Majesty and Electoral Highness went to the Habsburg court, and an Imperial and royal envoy to the Court of St James's.

At least, thanks to a long-running dispute over precedence, the above exchange could only take place after 1740. During the preceding decades, the Emperor Charles VI declined to deal with the Imperial electors, including Brunswick-Lüneburg, who had gained royal status on the side and were trying to present themselves as his equals.

Nonetheless, George Augustus was in the happy position of having two diplomatic services at his disposal. British diplomats rightly suspected him of bypassing the British secretaries of state, and his German ministers of letting London's policies prevail. On occasion, as in Vienna in the 1740s, royal and electoral diplomats signed their despatches jointly, sending copies both to London and to Hanover.[63] Without scrutinizing their credentials, it was sometimes unclear who was on a British errand and who not. The king-elector despatched whomsoever he thought appropriate. In 1727–8, for example, he sent the Hanoverian Baron von Dieskau to Stockholm, replacing him in 1728 with the British MP Edward Finch. In that same period, he caused friction by appointing Friedrich von Fabrice as plenipotentiary to the Saxon court at Dresden and expecting him to represent both the Electorate and Great Britain.

Under George Augustus, the British foreign-policy establishment was not entirely confined to the central core of dukes and belted earls. Some young aristocrats, like George Hervey, Earl of Bristol (1721–75), could step straight from the army into an ambassadorial role at Turin. More usually, promising young men would first serve as embassy secretaries. Such was the route to advancement of Thomas Robinson, 1st Baron Grantham (1695–1770), ambassador in Vienna from 1730 to 1748; of Sir Horace Mann (1706–86), who served in Florence for almost fifty years; of Arthur Villettes (1706–76), British resident in Turin, and minister plenipotentiary to the Helvetic Cantons from 1750 to 1765; and of Sir James Gray (1708–73), ambassador in Venice from 1746 to 1752 and in Naples from 1753 to 1763.

Similarly, ex-ambassadors were well placed to step up to the office of secretary of state. William Stanhope, Earl of

Harrington (1683–1756), ex-ambassador in Madrid, served from 1730 to 1742 as Secretary of State for the Southern Department; Robert Darcy, Earl of Holderness (1718–78), ex-ambassador in Venice, served throughout the 1750s as Secretary of State first for the Southern and then for the Northern Department. In 1755, when the Duke of Newcastle promoted Thomas Robinson to a secretaryship, Pitt remarked: 'The Duke might as well have sent us his jackboot.'[64]

In the eighteenth century there were two sorts of envoy: 'residents' holding permanent posts abroad, and 'plenipotentiaries extraordinary' sent on specific missions. Diplomatic rules demanded reciprocity, and the severance of relations during wars.[65] In peacetime, George Augustus normally maintained permanent residents in a dozen European courts, from Paris, Madrid and Vienna to Berlin, Dresden, St Petersburg and Constantinople. An accredited electoral representative to Bavaria and the Imperial Diet shuttled between Munich and Regensburg. Their business, largely conducted in French, was political, commercial and military. Top, hand-picked men were sent to Paris, including: up to 1730 Robert Walpole's brother, Horatio, Baron Wolterton; from 1730 to 1740 James, Earl Waldegrave, a relative of Walpole's daughter; and from 1748 to 1754 Lieutenant-General Willem van Keppel, Earl of Albemarle. One could also mention Sir Benjamin Keene, another Walpole protégé, who served in Madrid from 1729 to 1739 and 1748 to 1757; Onslow Burrish, ambassador to the Spanish Netherlands and from 1745 to 1758 in Munich; William de Nassau-Zuylestein, Earl of Rochford, from 1749 ambassador in Turin; and the Scotsman Sir Andrew Mitchell, who held a key post at the court of Frederick the Great from 1755 to 1765. The king-elector's longest-serving diplomat, Walter Titley, spent thirty-eight years in the embassy at Copenhagen.

Charles Hanbury Williams, MP (1708–59) was one of the era's more colourful diplomats.[66] A Welshman picked out by the king-elector, he served from 1747 to 1750 in Dresden and Berlin, and from 1752 to 1758 in St Petersburg. Expelled from Berlin, he declared his life there to be 'worse than that of a monkey on the island of Borneo'; and in Russia he famously engineered the romance between the future Tsarina Catherine and the future Polish king, Stanislaw Poniatowski. He also wrote poetry:

> Old England mourns her past disgrace,
> Sad fate of her unhappy race,
> By gibbets, gaols and axes.
> Th'inglorious slaughter war has made,
> Her rising debts, her sinking trade,
> Her places, pensions, taxes.
> Cross'd with such cares, press'd with such pains,
> What wonder if she thus complains,
> Tells thus her dismal story!
> In hopes, some wise, some patriot chief,
> Some statesmen born for her relief,
> Might yet retrieve her glory.[67]

Williams was backing Pitt.

Instructions to the king-elector's diplomats stressed their duty to protect their master's standing, to forge alliances and to prepare treaties. In 1728–9, by the Convention of

Prado and other meetings, they ended the Spanish war. In 1731, two Treaties of Vienna promoted the Pragmatic Sanction, and in 1745 the Treaty of Warsaw rallied support for Maria Theresa. The Treaties of St Petersburg (1747) and Aix-la-Chapelle (1748) terminated the War of the Austrian Succession. In 1756, the Treaty of Westminster, with Prussia, precipitated the Diplomatic Revolution and the Seven Years War.

In his personal dealings, George Augustus was far from diplomatic. 'The diplomat who says "Yes" means "Maybe",' Prince Talleyrand was to explain; 'the diplomat who says "Maybe" means "No", and the diplomat who says "No" is no diplomat.'[68] Yet the king-elector instinctively said 'No'. Even so, as wars dragged on, the little man at the head of the royal and electoral diplomatic services steadily won respect. 'Whatever may be thought of ... King George,' wrote a political opponent in 1755, 'he was perfectly skilled in all the recesses of that political labyrinth which forms the system of Germany; he had been brought up with it ... and was naturally a zealous asserter of his liberties.'[69]

WAR

Warrior princes, such as George Augustus, were preparing for war all their lives. He was trained for a world where sovereign rulers, like Charles XII or Frederick the Great, lived by the sword and risked dying by it. Wars supplied the test of manhood and morality; honour and courage counted above everything. 'Hanover the Brave' of Oudenarde had a reputation to uphold.

Moreover, to see the wars of his reign as he did, one must accept that Great Britain was less powerful than it later became and the Electorate more substantial than usually assumed. Britain's naval ascendancy was long incomplete;[70] to confront the major powers of the day, the king-elector needed the combined forces of all his realms.

The king-elector's closest advisers obviously understood that the physical separation of his insular and continental dominions posed problems. From the 1740s, however, when France reverted to its traditional adversarial role, Great Britain and the Electorate faced the same enemy, and could be expected to pull together. From the king-elector's viewpoint, it seemed natural that his British subjects should assist the Electorate in its hour of need, and vice-versa.

In thirty-three years, George Augustus was engaged in five wars, two of them caused by British interests and three by fears for the Electorate. He enjoyed peace for less time than he spent at war.

The Anglo-Spanish War of 1726–9 carried over from his father's reign, and the king-elector left his British ministers to extricate him. The fighting was inglorious. The Royal Navy failed in Panama. The Spanish blockade of Gibraltar flopped. At the Treaty of Seville, the 'most Serene King of Great Britain', the 'Most Christian King' (of France) and 'the Catholic King of Spain' agreed to 'a sincere and constant friendship'. George Augustus was acting in his capacity as king but not as elector.[71]

The War of the Polish Succession of 1733–8 arose from the death of the Saxon elector-king, Augustus II. Emperor Charles VI ordered his vassal, George Augustus, to help contest the imposition of a French-sponsored candidate. Walpole argued that his master's Imperial obligations did not apply, and British-Hanoverian involvement remained nominal. Eventually, with Russian backing, the emperor's Saxon candidate, Augustus III, prevailed; the French candidate, Stanislas Leszczynski, was compensated with Lorraine, and Francis, Duke of Lorraine (Maria Theresa's husband), with Tuscany.[72]

George Augustus was well advised to stay clear of Poland's wars, but can only have been fascinated from afar – not to say horrified – by the activities of several dramatis personae, unknown perhaps in Britain, but quite familiar to himself. His childhood lessons in genealogy came alive. His immediate Saxon neighbour, Augustus III (1696–1763), propped up by the Russians, was a central figure in the conflict. The dynastic marriages of his other neighbours, the Guelph dukes of Brunswick-Wolfenbüttel, involved them too. Peter the Great's grandson, Tsar Peter II (r. 1727–30) was the son of a princess of Brunswick-Wolfenbüttel. A powerful German faction in St Petersburg, dominated by Saxons and Wolfenbüttels, opposed the Tsarina Anna (r. 1730–40), whose principal military commander was the phenomenal Irish Jacobite Peter de Lacy (1678–1751). Anthony-Ulrich von Brunswick-Wolfenbüttel (1714–74), sent to Russia in 1733 to marry the Grand Duchess Anna Leopoldovna, was the father of the short-lived child-Tsar, Ivan VI (r. 1740–41) and co-regent of Russia, before falling foul of the violent coup organized by the Tsarina Elizabeth Petrovna (r. 1741–61). Prior to that, promoted by the German faction, Anthony-Ulrich's younger brother, the future Field Marshal

Ludwig-Ernst von Brunswick-Wolfenbüttel, took over the dukedom of the Russian-occupied Polish province of Courland, and was making matrimonial advances to Elizabeth Petrovna herself. Subsequently, everything went sour for them in Russia, but, as dynastic adventurers, the Wolfenbüttel Guelphs came within an ace of overtaking the Hanoverian Guelphs.

The War of the Asiento, known to the British as the War of Jenkins' Ear, erupted in 1739 from the old Anglo-Spanish dispute over Caribbean trading rights. France stood aloof. The Royal Navy sent expeditions to South America, and colonists clashed in British Georgia and Spanish Florida. In 1741-3, Admiral Anson circumnavigated the globe, returning with a vast Spanish treasure from which the famous 'Lima' coinage was minted. By then, intermittent warfare had merged into a wider continental conflagration.[73]

The War of the Austrian Succession of 1740–48, sparked by the Emperor Charles VI's death and the invocation of the Pragmatic Sanction, aroused the king-elector's deepest concerns. Unlike his nephew, Frederick of Prussia, who treacherously invaded the Imperial province of Silesia, George Augustus did not openly renege on his duty to the Habsburgs, though he did evade the initial call to arms; by giving political support to the Bavarians, he helped install Charles VII von Wittelsbach as emperor. He was only spurred into military action by a French offensive into Germany in 1742–3. The Pragmatic Army, which he led, revived youthful memories of the Grand Alliance.[74] He and his allies, consisting of electoral, British, Imperial, Hessian and Dutch troops, aimed to protect Hanover by pushing the

French back to the Rhine. To this end, he caught up with their main force at Dettingen-am-Main near Frankfurt, and on 27 June 1743 drew them into battle. Bravely riding along the front line wearing the yellow sash of Brunswick, he roused the spirit of his multinational regiments and won a signal victory. 'The French fired at his Majesty from a battery of twelve cannon,' said a witness. 'I saw the balls go within half a yard of his head.' Told to take cover, he replied, 'Don't tell me of danger; I'll be even with them.'[75] In Parliament, William Pitt fumed that England was shackled to a 'despicable Electorate'.[76]

In response, Versailles determined to clip the king-elector's wings by organizing a Jacobite rising in Scotland. The 'Forty-Five' could not have happened otherwise. 'Bonnie Prince Charlie' landed at Moidart in the Western Highlands in August 1745 and roused the clans. Edinburgh welcomed him, and his growing army defeated a loyalist force at Prestonpans before marching south. The Highlanders occupied a wintry Manchester, but, lacking English support, turned back at Derby.[77] Urged to flee, the king-elector exclaimed ungrammatically: 'Pooh! Don't talk to me that stuff!' before personally establishing a military camp on Finchley Common for London's defence. (Hogarth marked the event in a satirical painting, *The March to Finchley*, which the monarch refused to buy.[78]) Urged by privy councillors to be more cautious, he told them: 'Gentlemen, take care of yourselves!'[79]

In 1746, the retreating Jacobites were mercilessly harried by an army led by William, Duke of Cumberland. On the dismal moor of Culloden, near Inverness, the Highlanders made their last charge armed with claymores, only to be slaughtered by the superior firepower of royal and electoral regiments.[80] The Young Pretender took to the heather:

> Speed, bonnie boat, like a bird on the wing,
> Onward, the sailors cry.
> Carry the lad that's born to be king
> Over the sea to Skye.[81]

The 'Forty-Five' sealed the fate both of Gaelic civilization, which was crushed, and of the Hanoverian Guelphs, who were never to be challenged in Britain again. 'The most savage barbarities were committed', noted a contemporary, 'that ever disgraced humanity or ever Englishmen were guilty of,' adding that the king-elector 'neither commanded nor approved of them'.[82] The Jacobites sang their bitter and beautiful laments:

> Will ye no come back again?
> Will ye no come back again?
> Better lo'ed ye canna be.
> Will ye no come back again?[83]

And the loyalists sang 'God Save the King'.

Among those loyalists, the Jewish financier Sampson Gideon was especially prominent. Scoring a major financial coup in the panic of 1745 by buying up underpriced stocks,[84] he was credited with using the money to bankroll Cumberland's Culloden campaign. He then lobbied Pelham's government for a Jewish Naturalisation Bill, to which George Augustus gave his assent in 1753. The Jewish Naturalisation Act briefly enabled Jews to apply to Parliament for British citizenship. Within a year, however, thanks to a Tory-led uproar over 'the abandonment of Christianity', it was repealed.

The main war, meanwhile, had spread to North America, India and Italy. In the Low Countries, the French advanced to the Dutch border after triumphing at Fontenoy, where British and Hanoverian troops fought side by side, but were bettered by the rebel Irish Brigade serving in the French ranks. The Treaty of Aix-la-Chapelle of 1748 confirmed Francis I's appointment as emperor, Frederick II's hold on Silesia, and the Protestant Succession in Britain.[85] George Augustus was reasonably content.

The Seven Years War of 1756–63 rekindled hostilities after a startling reversal of international alignments. In January 1756, by the Westminster Convention, George Augustus made common cause with his estranged Prussian nephew, Frederick, agreeing to support Prussia's possession of Silesia in return for Prussian protection of Hanover. Maria Theresa reacted by courting both the French and the Russians, and the two king-electors were left facing a new combination of Vienna, Paris and St Petersburg.[86] This Diplomatic Revolution is usually presented as the balance of power in action. From George Augustus's standpoint, it marked the moment when he abandoned his lifelong Imperial loyalty and adopted the Prussian example of pursuing total independence. If Pitt's Patriots had noticed, they should have rejoiced.[87]

French and British colonists clashed in America, before France reopened European proceedings in June 1756 with an attack on British-held Minorca. Frederick then invaded

France's ally, Saxony, prompting a chain reaction engulfing almost every state in Europe.[88] George Augustus was involved in two ways: firstly by waging global war against France by land and sea, and secondly by forming an Allied Army of Observation to guard the Electorate. Hard-pressed by rival factions, he reluctantly agreed to invite Pitt to join his government.[89]

In the king-elector's eyes, 1757 brought unprecedented disaster. Despite vast British subsidies, Prussia reneged on its obligations, pulling back the troops that were shielding the Electorate. Pitt was dismissed, then reinstated. A French army forded the Weser, broke through the Electorate's diminished defences and occupied Hanover. By the Convention of Klosterzeven, Cumberland was forced to accept neutrality and withdrew his multinational Army of Observation. Here was the calamity which had always terrified the Hanoverian Guelphs. The French not only perpetrated the usual extortions; they installed an official Parisian tax-farmer in Hanover 'pour piller méthodiquement'.[90] George Augustus denounced the Convention and replaced Cumberland with Ferdinand, Duke of Brunswick (Fat Louis's brother).

In 1758 the gloom lifted. In French eyes, Hanover's suffering led the British, who disliked '*la guerre de terre*', to change tack and to send reinforcements. '*Le grand* Pitt' brilliantly declared: 'We shall win Canada on the banks of the Elbe.' British and Hanoverian interests were at last in sync. Ferdinand of Brunswick, 'qui réunisse tous les talens sublimes', moved to the offensive.[91] Good news of the war came from Bengal, from Canadian Louisbourg, from Rossbach in

Saxony, and finally from Hanover. The French were evacu-
ating the Electorate.

The British acclaimed 1759 as 'the year of victories'. The
Royal Navy was subduing the world's oceans. George Augustus's music master composed the navy's theme song:

> Hearts of Oak are our ships,
> Hearts of Oak are our men.
> We always ready,
> Steady, boys, steady!
> We'll fight and we'll conquer again and again.[92]

A fleet of 170 warships sailed up the St Lawrence carrying
General James Wolfe's expeditionary force to Quebec.

James Wolfe's lifespan (1727–59) was almost exactly the
same as the king-elector's reign. He had joined the Marines
as a boy-soldier, fought at Dettingen and Culloden, and
famously refused an order to shoot a wounded Highlander.
On the eve of battle on the Heights of Abraham above
Quebec, where he would die, he read to his troops from
Gray's 'Elegy'.[93]

George Augustus closely watched all who served him. Of
Admiral Byng, court-martialled for abandoning Minorca, he
said: 'This man will not fight'; and, with the mob chanting
'Swing, swing, Admiral Byng', confirmed the death sentence.[94]
Voltaire famously quipped that the English occasionally kill
an admiral *pour encourager les autres*. In contract, the king-
elector defended Wolfe to the hilt. When the Duke of
Newcastle dared to say that Wolfe was 'mad' for sparing the
Highlander, he retorted: 'Mad is he? I hope that he will bite
some of my other generals.'[95]

By 1760, therefore, the ageing monarch could relax. His strategies were working. Peace was elusive, but the nightmare had passed. His kingdoms were secure; his Electorate had returned to the fold. He could safely exit the stage.

8

Dusk

Reaching the biblical threescore years and ten in 1753, George Augustus slowed down. He lost the sight of one eye and much of his hearing, and suffered from haemorrhoids, from chest pains, and from worryingly frequent coughs and colds. Impatient and irritable, he kept advancing age at bay through a strict routine of early rising, saying his German prayers, eating a hearty breakfast, horse-riding when weather permitted, taking a siesta, wearing simpler clothes,[1] and receiving his ministers in audience. In the evenings he would dress for dinner, visit the theatre or preside at court gatherings.

Ever since the queen-electress's death, the climate at court had changed. George Augustus's generation was ageing with him. At Kensington, Amalie von Wallmoden and her associates were in the ascendant. Criticism of the monarch was stifled. In the 1750s, as Horace Walpole reported, a discernible shift of tone was in progress:

> I am sensible that from the prostitution of patriotism, from the art of ministers . . . and from the bent of the education of young nobility, which verges to French maxims and to a military spirit . . . , prerogative and power have been exceedingly fortified of late within the circle of the palace.[2]

All the while, the memoirists were collecting the bilious stories that would damage the king-elector's future reputation. John Hervey, Earl of Bristol (1696–1743), a vice-chamberlain, a bisexual, a gossip-monger and a special friend of Princess Charlotte, had been active in the early years. Portrayed by Pope as 'Lord Fanny', he barely survived a duel provoked by his pamphlet *Sedition and Defamation Display'd* (1731). His voluminous manuscripts languished unpublished until Victorian times.[3]

Horace Walpole (1717–97), the ex-prime minister's son, continued where Hervey left off. An aesthete, a wealthy sinecurist and a 'hermaphrodite horse' by one description, he returned in 1741 from the Grand Tour, got himself elected an absentee MP, collected pictures, built the precocious neo-Gothic villa at Strawberry Hill, wrote novels and art history, cruised the salons and gathered anecdotes. No admirer of the king-elector, he preyed on his every foible. 'This world is a comedy to those who think,' he concluded, 'and a tragedy to those who feel.' His vast correspondence, like Hervey's, was only published posthumously.[4] He was brilliant but an untrustworthy source, with a 'strong vein of malice'.[5]

In 1752, George II Augustus took the Duke of Newcastle with him to Hanover, and three years later returned there with the Earl of Holderness and Archbishop Herring in tow.[6] His daughter Mary came over from Hanau to pass a sunny summer with him.[7] Fearful that his nephew Frederick might visit Herrenhausen, he conferred with his chief minister, von Münchhausen, convened his electoral Privy Council and strengthened the Electorate's defences. He made mercenary deals with Caroline's relative, the 'Wild Margrave' of Ansbach, and with his son-in-law at Hesse-Kassel. On Sunday evenings, at the customary assembly of nobles, the company stood up dutifully to sing the electoral anthem to the melody of 'God Save the King':

> Heil Dir Hannover, heil!
> Freude werd' Dir zuteil,
> Freude stets mehr.
> Jauchze, Du Engelschor,
> Dringe zu Gottes Ohr!
> Mit Deinem Freudenchor:
> Gebt Gott die Ehr.[8]

The composite state, it seems, had twin anthems.

Back in London, the king-elector was preoccupied by the rapprochement with Prussia – stressful for him, popular with the public – and by diplomatic flurries round the signing in January 1756 of the Convention of Westminster.[9] In February he watched the launch at Woolwich of the 100-gun HMS *Royal George*, the largest warship in the world.[10] He would soon present a declaration of war to his enemies, bristling with indignation:

The unwarrantable proceedings of the French in the West Indies ... and [their] usurpations and encroachments ... in Nova Scotia, have been so notorious and so frequent that they cannot but be looked upon as evidence of a formed Design ... without any regard to the most solemn Treaties and Engagements ... We, therefore, ... do hereby declare war against the French King ... relying on the Help of

Almighty God ... and being assured of the hearty concur-
rence ... of our subjects; hereby willing Our Captain of our
Force ... by Sea and by Land, to do and execute all acts of
Hostility ... Given at our Court at Kensington, the 17th day
of May 1756 in the 29th year of our reign.[11]

By this time, George Augustus might have guessed that a
ministerial showdown was likely. Yet, as he knew with
greater certainty, wars with France provided an important
part of the cement which bound Great Britain and Hanover
together. And so it proved. In 1757, having once dismissed
Pitt and restored him, he buried their differences. Yet he
kept Pitt in his place – literally. He granted him audiences
during his siesta, inviting him to kneel on a cushion on the
floor at his bedside.[12]

On 21 July 1759, James Woodforde, an Oxford student,
made the first entry in an extraordinary diary. He went on to
be a country parson in Norfolk, recording all the daily events,
colourful characters, men, women and animals, food and
drink, joys, ordeals and sorrows of rural life. A classic of
Georgian England, it started in George Augustus's time, but
in a space that he never knew.[13]

Between 1751 and 1759, George Augustus wrote and
amended his last will and testament. The king-elector's will
of 3 April 1751 had been prompted by Prince Frederick's
death, and superseded all earlier versions. It named Prince
George as his successor, and settled some 3.3 million *Reich-
sthaler* on Cumberland. The codicil of 6 October 1757,
drawn up after Cumberland's poor recent performance as

commander, significantly reduced his bequest, and made provision for supporting 'our military Establishment in Germany'. Having made some minor amendments after the recovery of Hanover, the monarch deposited one copy with the electoral Privy Council, another with the court in Celle, a third with Princess Amelia in London, and none with the British authorities.[14]

9
Decease

In 1760, aged seventy-seven, George Augustus was surrounded in London by cheering crowds. The public mood was near-euphoric. Odes on the victories of the previous year were in vogue:

> Blow the trumpet, strike the lyre,
> British hearts with joy inspire.
> Voice with instruments combine
> To praise the glorious Fifty-nine![1]

On New's Year's Day, 'Hearts of Oak' received its première at the Theatre Royal, Drury Lane, together with another rousing song:

> In Story we're told,
> How our Monarchs of old,
> O'er France spread their Royal Domain.
> But no annals shall shew
> Her pride laid so low
> As when George the Second did reign, brave boys,
> When brave George the Second did reign.[2]

British ships, British guns and British money were carrying all before them.

Taking stock, George Augustus and his entourage had more mixed feelings. For, as Great Britain rapidly turned into a world power, the Electorate's fate still wavered. Overall, however, there was reason for quiet satisfaction. At Minden on the Weser the previous August, it was British regiments which had tipped the balance and again saved Hanover from the French.[3] Compared to the Hohenzollerns, the Wettins, the Hesse-Kassels and the Habsburgs, not to mention the Stuarts, the Hanoverian Guelphs were not doing too badly.

The monarch's duplicitous nephew Frederick was now facing annihilation. At the Battle of Kunersdorf, which had coincided with Minden, the boastful Prussians had been pulverized by Russian power. The Elector-king of Saxony had virtually abandoned his Polish kingdom, which would be definitively lost after his death in 1763, and the Hesse-Kassels had lost Sweden long since.[4] The Habsburg Empire was under attack from all sides. And the wretched Stuarts had dropped from sight. Bonnie Prince Charlie, expelled from France, was submitting to drink. His last disastrous interview with French ministers in 1759 persuaded them to cancel a contemplated invasion of Britain.

In fact, the best expectations of the king-elector's early reign were being exceeded. His realms were expanding; his throne was secure; the Protestant ascendancy thrived; his kingdoms were working well with the Electorate; and the whole ramshackle contraption of Great Britain-Hanover, having outpaced the era's other dynastic composites, was intact. He had fallen short on his sworn loyalty to the Holy Roman Empire. Yet Maria Theresa's alliance with France to some extent exculpated him. Honour was not lost.

As 1760 unfolded, the war news was generally positive. British arms had triumphed in both India and Canada, though on the continent Prussian and Hanoverian fortunes were in see-saw mode. Animated press comment was aroused when 'an assembly of brethren called Quakers' took up the old Patriotic argument about Great Britain fighting the French at sea but not on land. Yet most observers now saw Britain's interest in opposing France on all fronts. In April, the court martial of Lord George Sackville, a cavalry commander charged with disobeying orders at Minden, hit the headlines. The defendant, outraged by talk of cowardice, had demanded the hearing himself, only to receive a unique judgment:

> Upon due consideration . . . [it is this court's] opinion, THAT Lord George Sackville is guilty of having disobeyed the orders of Prince Ferdinand of Brunswick . . . according to the rules of war: and [further] . . . THAT the said Lord George Sackville . . . is hereby adjudged unfit to serve his Majesty in any military capacity whatsoever.[5]

On confirming the sentence publicly, George Augustus added a characteristic warning: for 'a man of honour', he said, there could be 'censures much worse than death'.[6]

That same month, a brief account was also published of colonial negotiations in Georgia 'between Governor Lyttleton and Attakullakulla [the Little Carpenter], deputee of the Cherokee nation'. 'It is the will of the Great King', the governor announced, 'that his people and your people should live together in friendship.'[7] George Augustus loved being called 'the Great King'.

In May, a minor sensation occurred within a stone's throw of the king-elector's residence: Earl Ferrers, who had murdered his steward, was hanged on a silk rope at Tyburn. Pardon had been withheld.[8]

The results of the summer campaigning season were ambivalent. The Prussians, popular with the British public, battled the Austrians in Silesia but left Berlin undefended. On the Electorate's borders, the Duke of Brunswick led the Allied army in July into a successful engagement at Warburg, again thwarting French designs. The British contingent, especially the Marquis of Granby, whose hat and wig blew off during the cavalry charge, covered itself in glory. Less pleasingly, French raiders seized the 'Wild Margrave's' capital of Cassel and raced on to capture Göttingen.

George Augustus's domestic worries remained unresolved. He was dismayed at Cumberland's military failures, disappointed that Anne's widowed husband, the Prince of Orange, had not joined the war, and concerned for Mary, who had fled with her children from Cassel to Hamburg. Princess Amelia, a middle-aged spinster, was the only child left at home to comfort him. He was mourning his old friend and servant, the Duke of Grafton, who had long formed a courtly triumvirate with Amelia and himself. He was disturbed by William Pitt's unwelcome association with Princess Augusta and her mentor, John Stuart, Earl of Bute (1713–92), who were blocking his plans for Prince George's marriage; and he was driven to distraction by Pitt's brother-in-law, Richard Grenville, Earl Temple (1711–79), Lord Privy Seal, who was shamelessly angling for the Garter.[9]

The first three weeks of October 1760 passed uneventfully. George Augustus undoubtedly sat up on hearing that the Russians had occupied Berlin; all his calculations about the war in Germany were based on the alliance with Prussia.[10] But readers of the *Gentleman's Magazine* were mostly treated to a stream of mundane events:

Monday 20. His Majesty attended by the royal family reviewed Col. Burgoyne's regiment of light dragoons from a tent in Hyde Park . . .

Thursday 23. This morning, the third battalion of the First Regiment of Foot marched from the Tower to Portsmouth in three divisions. His Majesty was in the portico of Kensington Palace to see them pass by.[11]

Then, on the morning of Saturday 25 October, the fatal blow fell without warning:

[George II Augustus] rose, as usual, at six o'clock. He called for his hot chocolate . . . He then walked over to the window overlooking the gardens . . . and declared . . . he would [go for a] walk. A little after seven o'clock, he retreated into the water-closet, methodical as ever . . . His *valet de chambre* [Schröder] waiting patiently outside . . . was surprised by a sound 'louder than the royal wind' followed by a thud 'like a billet of wood falling from the fire'. He rushed in to find the [king-elector] lying on the floor – a gash on his right temple . . . and his hand stretched towards the bell to ring for assistance. He whispered 'Call Amelia', then spoke no more.[12]

All attempts to revive the stricken monarch failed. A post-mortem would reveal that 'the right ventricle of the heart was burst' and 'the key of his bureau was found in his hand'.[13] Amalie von Wallmoden, clutching her strongbox, was callously expelled from her apartments.[14] And William Pitt, a coach-and-pair at the ready, rushed off, just as Robert Walpole had done thirty-three years earlier, to tell Prince George of his succession.

10
Legacy

On the day of the monarch's death, one of the copies of his will was opened by a small group of beneficiaries: Prince George, the Duke of Cumberland, Princess Amelia and Philipp von Münchhausen. Its preamble rejected any fragmentation of the 'Firm's' assets. Prince George was to inherit all his grandfather's realms. Though reduced, the sums of money bequeathed to Cumberland were still large; lesser gifts were left to Amelia, Caroline, Ernst von Steinberg, Gerlach Adolph von Münchhausen and Amalie von Wallmoden.[1] The latter came away with the loose cash.[2]

Thereupon, news of the decease was sent to Hanover; Prince George's accession was proclaimed and the British Privy Council summoned. On receiving their oaths of allegiance, the new king-elector addressed the councillors:

> The loss that I and the nation have sustained . . . would have been severely felt at any time – but . . . the weight now falling upon me [is] much increased. I feel my own insufficiency . . . But animated by the tenderest affection for my native country . . . I shall make it the business of my life to promote the glory and happiness of these kingdoms.[3]

The shift in tone was apparent, the emphasis on 'my native country' unmistakable. Office holders were told to keep their posts 'pending His Majesty's pleasure'.

The Earl Marshal then ordered general mourning; ladies were to wear 'black bombazines, plain muslin, and crape hoods', gentlemen 'black cloth without buttons, crape hat-bands, and black swords and buckles'. Hanover was to follow suit. The funeral, held on 11 November in Westminster Abbey, started with a grand procession lined by thousands of guardsmen.[4] The Duke of Cumberland acted as chief mourner. The Dukes of Newcastle and Bridgewater carried his train. William Boyce's funerary anthem rang out: 'The souls of the righteous are in God's hands.' Horace Walpole noted that 'the [abbey] was so illuminated that the tombs, long aisles and fretted roof all appeared with the happiest chiaroscuro.'

George Augustus was laid to rest alongside his late wife in the Hanoverian vault in the crypt. One side of the sarcophagus was left open so that his remains could mingle with Caroline's:

The Royal corps being interred, the Dean of Westminster [recited] the office of burial, and a Garter of Arms proclaimed his late Majesty's stile: 'Thus it has pleased Almighty God to take ... to his divine mercy the late most high, most mighty and most excellent monarch, GEORGE the IId, by the Grace of God, King ... Defender of the Faith, Sovereign of the Most Noble Order of the Garter, Duke of Brunswick and Lunenburgh ... Elector of the Holy Roman Empire.[5]

Inexplicably, no public gravestone or monument was ever erected – as if thirty-three years of history were consigned to oblivion. Present-day visitors to the abbey admire elaborate memorials to George Augustus's musician, Handel. Yet, except for the initials 'GR' inscribed on one small tile in the Lady Chapel's floor, they find no trace of the monarch himself. Over the centuries since his death, the personality and reputation of George Augustus have rarely been celebrated. Few commentators recount the blessings of his reign.

The opinions of British contemporaries were often ambiguous. Lord Berkeley of Stratton, Princess Amelia's friend, wrote that her father was 'a good prince, if not an amiable man'. Lord Chesterfield thought that he was 'a weak, rather than a bad king'. And Horace Walpole made positive and negative assessments in quick succession:

> The King had fewer sensations of revenge . . . than any man that ever sat upon a throne. The insults he experienced . . . never [seriously] provoked him . . . He was reckoned strictly honest, but the burning of his father's will must be an indelible blot on his memory . . . His avarice was [overstated, and] his understanding was not so near deficient as imagined . . . Though so much ridiculed in [his early years] and so much respected [later], he was consistent of himself . . . His other passions were Germany, the Army, and women . . .[6]

Thereupon, Walpole launched into a second passage comparing the monarch unfavourably with his predecessors: 'He had the haughtiness of Henry VIII without his spirit: the avarice of Henry VII without his exactions . . . the vexatiousness of King William, with as little skill in the management of parties, and the gross gallantry of his father, without his good nature and honesty.'[7]

Yet more generous views were not lacking. 'Upon the whole,' said the younger Lord Waldegrave, '[George Augustus] has some qualities of a great prince, many of a good one, and none which are essentially bad.'[8] 'I have known few persons of high rank,' he added tellingly, 'who could take contradiction better.'[9] Lord Hardwicke wrote: 'He died in the height of his glory, loved, honoured and respected by all Europe.'[10] Even William Pitt forgot former hostilities. 'The late, good old King had something of humanity,' he recalled, 'and possessed justice, truth and sincerity in an eminent degree.'[11] Nobody in Britain thought to compare him with other contemporary sovereigns.

Pitt's generosity was reflected in other obituaries by former critics:

[The king-elector's] mien was majestic, and he wore age so extremely well . . . In temper, he was sudden and violent . . . However . . . [in] disposition he was merciful, and on numberless occasions humane . . . He appears with greatest lustre as a soldier . . . To say that he was perfectly acquainted with our constitution . . . would be as to say he perfectly knew our language. [But] . . . his government seldom deviated from the established forms of law.[12]

John Almon concluded on a high note:

[George Augustus] lived to see the spirit of party extinguished . . . to [have] his family firmly seated on the throne,

to experience ... his people's affections and to see ... the
power of his kingdoms raised to an [unexpected] pitch ...
He was an enemy to no religion [and] he did not molest the
free and full exercise ... of the human mind ... This mildness
and toleration will endear a respect to his memory ...'

One can only speculate why these laudatory opinions were
destined to fade. But fade they did, and quickly. Long before
the end of the century, George Augustus's achievements were
either ignored or discounted. One reason can be summed by
the oft-repeated phrase: 'his partiality for his [foreign]
dominions'. Another undoubtedly lay in the rise of the Whig
Interpretation of History, which habitually degraded monarchs to the greater glory of Parliament.[13]

Historians and biographers have always bemoaned the
paucity of sources, and sometimes regurgitate unverified
judgements. Yet their besetting sin has probably been
anachronism – judging an early-eighteenth-century ruler by
the yardsticks of later times. They wrongly assume that the
monarchy's decline, the supremacy of Parliament and the
anglicization of the Georgian Establishment were far
advanced. In Germany, where history-writing became preoccupied with Prussia, the Hanoverian Guelphs were
relegated to the margins of provincial history.

In Britain, the 'Georges' weren't completely erased from
the historical narrative, but they were routinely disparaged.
'All too often,' writes one of their few defenders, 'George I
and George II are seen as grumpy, German and indistin-
guishable,'[14] or as 'bad', 'sad', 'mad' and 'fat'.[15] George
Augustus finds no niche in the national pantheon of *1066*

and All That.[16] And, in the hands of Macaulay, Froude, Green, Stubbs and Trevelyan, the Whig Interpretation denigrated anyone who spoiled its teleological scheme of constitutional progress. Historians of the English patriotic tendency, meanwhile, harped on about George Augustus's Germanic pedantry, merrily mocking the absurd notion that 'the safety of Hanover' could be as important as 'the wishes of England': 'His mind was incapable of rising above the merest details of business. He made war in the spirit of a drill-sergeant, and economised his income with the minute regularity of a clerk ... He took the greatest pleasure in counting his money ... and he never forgot a date.'[17]

Pejorative adjectives multiplied: 'dull', 'dim-witted', 'petulant', 'devoid of originality', 'haughty', 'tetchy', 'pompous', 'ludicrous', 'vain', 'dressy', 'excitingly dysfunctional' and 'stupid but complicated'.[18] Learned scholars descended into slapstick, calling George Augustus everything from 'a man in toils' and 'a wash-out' to a 'tin-pot dictator' and a 'nincompoop'.[19] The Victorian doggerel stuck:

> George the First was always reckon'd
> Vile, viler George the Second.[20]

Rescuing the king-elector from this torrent of gratuitous invective is difficult. 'The considered judgement of most who worked with him', wrote one brave biographer, 'was a great deal better than the cursory treatment accorded him by historians.'[21] More recently, a Cambridge scholar has gone further, rising above the Anglocentric tumult and placing 'the forgotten king' firmly into the wider European context. Andrew Thompson's full biography sports the subtitle 'King and Elector', signalling 'the dual nature of his kingship', detailing his notable contribution to foreign policy and firing off many positive adjectives – from 'active', 'knowledgeable' and 'capable', to 'skilful', 'adaptable', 'powerful', 'canny' and 'conscientious'.[22] No one suggests that George Augustus was faultless. But at long last, his royal and electoral personage is again recognized as a substantial international figure, and no longer stands in the dunce's corner.

In the strange absence of an official memorial to George II Augustus, therefore, it may be appropriate to cite a verse composed during his reign in the most serene of poems:

> Nor you, ye proud, impute to these the fault,
> If Mem'ry o'er their tomb no trophies raise,
> Where thro' the long-drawn aisle and fretted vault
> The pealing anthem swells the note of praise.[23]

Notes

PROLOGUE

1. Ragnhild Hatton, *George I: Elector and King* (New Haven, CT and London: Yale University Press, 2001), pp. 280–81.

NOTE ON LINGUISTIC TRANSPOSITIONS

1. Tracy Borman, *King's Mistress, Queen's Servant: The Life and Times of Henrietta Howard* (London: Vintage, 2010), p. 239.

1. 1683: THE WORLD OF GEORGE AUGUSTUS VON WELF

1. Andrew Halliday, *A General History of the House of Guelph or Royal Family of Great Britain . . .* (London, 1821), dedicated to 'George the Fourth, King of the United Kingdom and Ireland, King of the Kingdom of Hanover, Duke of Brunswick and Lüneburg etc.'.
2. From Robert Browning, 'The Pied Piper of Hamelin': <poetryfoundation.org/poems/45818/the-pied-piper-of-hamelin> (2017).
3. See J. W. Stoye, *The Siege of Vienna* (London: Collins, 1964).
4. See R. J. W. Evans, *The Making of the Holy Roman Empire, 1500–1700: An Interpretation* (Oxford: Clarendon Press, 1979); Martyn Rady, *The Habsburg Empire: A Very Short Introduction* (Oxford: Oxford University Press, 2017); Francis Carsten, *The Empire after the Thirty Years War* (Cambridge: Cambridge University Press, 1961).
5. See D. H. Pennington, *Seventeenth-Century Europe* (London: Longman, 1970).
6. See Christopher Clark, *Iron Kingdom: The Rise and Downfall of Prussia, 1600–1947* (London: Penguin, 2007); Derek McKay, *The Great Elector* (Harlow: Longman, 2001); Norman Davies, 'Borussia: Watery Land of the Prusai, 1230–1945', in *Vanished Kingdoms: The History of Half-Forgotten Europe* (London: Allen Lane, 2011), pp. 325–94.
7. Norman Davies, 'Wettin: The Saxon Era, 1697–1763', in *God's Playground: A History of Poland* (Oxford: Clarendon Press, 2000), vol. 1, pp. 370–85; Robert Frost, 'Some Hidden Thunder: Hanover, Saxony and the Management of Political Union, 1697–1763', in B. S. Sirota and A. I. Macinnes (eds), *The Hanoverian Succession in Great Britain and its Empire* (Martlesham: Boydell & Brewer, 2019), pp. 193–211.
8. Norman Davies, 'Sabaudia: The House that Humbert Built, 1033–1946', in *Vanished Kingdoms*, pp. 395–438.
9. See Knud Jespersen, *A History of Denmark* (London: Red Globe Press, 2018).

10. See Neil Kent, *A Concise History of Sweden* (Cambridge: Cambridge University Press, 2008).

11. See Antonia Fraser, *King Charles II* (London: Phoenix, 2002).

12. See J. N. Duggan, *Sophia of Hanover: From Winter Princess to Heiress of Great Britain* (London: Peter Owen, 2010).

13. Tim Blanning, *George I: The Lucky King* (London: Allen Lane, 2017), p. 8.

2. 1683–1714: THIRTY-ONE RUNGS OF THE LADDER

1. The principal biographies include: Charles Chenevix-Trench, *George II* (London: Allen Lane, 1973); Jeremy Black, *George II: Puppet of the Politicians?* (Exeter: University of Exeter Press, 2007) and most recently, Andrew Thompson, *George II: King and Elector* (New Haven, CT and London: Yale University Press, 2011). See also John Owen, 'George II Reconsidered', in A. Whiteman et al. (eds), *Essays Presented to Lucy Sutherland* (Oxford: Clarendon Press, 1973).

2. See Johannes Zahlten, *Herrenhausen. Die Sommerresidenz der Welfen* (Hanover: Feesche, 1966).

3. The characteristic trait of 'bad temper' or irascibility, which was to dog George Augustus to the end of his life, was discussed at some length by his grandmother, Duchess Sophie, in her correspondence with her niece, Liselotte of Orleans (see letter 608 of July 1706, quoted by Thompson, *George II*, p. 16), so it clearly was a matter for family concern.

4. See G. M. Thomson, *Warrior Prince: Prince Rupert of the Rhine* (London: Secker & Warburg, 1976).

5. See J. A. Lynn, *The Wars of Louis XIV, 1667–1714* (London: Longman, 1999).

6. See J. B. Wolf, *The Emergence of the Great Powers, 1685–1717* (New York: Harper & Bros, 1951).

7. See Steven Pincus, *England's Glorious Revolution, 1688–1689: A Brief History with Documents* (Basingstoke: Palgrave Macmillan, 2006).

8. Electorate of Brunswick-Lüneburg, <enacademic.com/dic.nsf/enwiki/11671820> (2020).

9. See David Ogg, *William III* (London: Collins, 1956).

10. 'Murdered by King George I?', <historyanswers.co.uk/kings-queens/murdered-on-the-orders-of-king-george-i> (2020); W. H. Wilkins, *The Love of an Uncrowned Queen* (London: Hutchinson, 1900, 2 vols).

11. Józef Gierowski and Andrzej Kaminski (trans. Norman Davies), 'The Eclipse of Poland', *New Cambridge Modern History*, vol. 6 (Cambridge: Cambridge University Press, 1970), pp. 681–715.

12. See James Falkner, *The War of the Spanish Succession, 1701–14* (Barnsley: Pen and Sword, 2015).

13. See Peter Englund, *The Battle that Shook Europe: Poltava and the Birth of the Russian Empire* (London: I. B. Tauris, 2003); Robert Frost, *The Northern Wars, 1558–1721* (London: Longman, 2000); H. Lunde, *Warrior Dynasty: The Rise and Decline of Sweden as a Military Superpower, 1611–1721* (Philadelphia, PA and Oxford: Casemate, 2014).

14. Act of Settlement: <archive.org/stream/statutesatlarge31Britgoog#page/n403/mode/2up> (2020).

15. W. Belsham, *History of Great Britain, from the revolution to the session of parliament ending AD 1793* (London, 1806), vol. 2, p. 199. Charles Gerard, 2nd Earl of Macclesfield

(1659–1701), whose father had landed at Torbay with William of Orange, was an English major-general. A former associate of the Duke of Monmouth, he had been sentenced to death in the wake of the Rye House Plot, but later reprieved.

16. Jonathan Swift, 'Victory Ode', quoted by Blanning, *George I*, p. 15.
17. See Peter Verney, *The Battle of Blenheim* (London: Batsford, 1976).
18. See Correlli Barnett, *Marlborough* (London: Methuen, 1974).
19. Andrew Hanham, 'The Duke of Cambridge and the Hanoverian Succession, 1706–14', History of Parliament Online, <histparl.ac.uk/periods/stuarts/duke-cambridge-and-hanoverian-succession-1706–14> (2020).
20. Act of Union, <en.wikisource.org/wiki/Act_of_Union_of_1701> (2020).
21. See Christopher Scott, *The Battle of Oudenarde* (Leigh-on-Sea: Partizan Press, 2008).The twenty-year-old James Edward Stuart, the Old Pretender, the Chevalier de Saint-Georges, also participated in the battle with distinction, making repeated charges in the ranks of the French household cavalry. But the two rival claimants to the British throne never met. Hostile accounts, which suggest that the Pretender watched the battle from a nearby steeple, have been discounted. See also Desmond Seward, *The King over the Water: The Jacobite Cause, 1688–1807* (Edinburgh: Birlinn, 2019).
22. Bremen and Verden (see Chapter 3, note 22 below).
23. Peace of Utrecht, <courseslumenlearning.com/suny-hccc-worldhistory/chapter/the-peace-of-utrecht> (2020).
24. William Coxe, *Memoirs of John, Duke of Marlborough* (London, 1820), vol. 6, pp. 261–2.
25. See Edward Gregg, *Queen Anne* (London: Routledge, 1980).
26. Queen Anne to the Dowager Duchess Sophia, 19 May 1701; Belsham, *History of Great Britain*, vol. 6, p. 710.
27. Ibid., pp. 526–7.

3. 1714–1727: APPRENTICESHIP

1. See Hatton, *George I*; Blanning, *George I*, 'The Hanoverian Succession in England', pp. 17–37.
2. See William Makepeace Thackeray, *The Four Georges* (London, 1861).
3. See Zoe Sharp, *Riot Act* (London: Piatkus, 2002); J. S. Monroe, *The Riot Act* (London: Head of Zeus, 2018).
4. See Borman, *King's Mistress*, chapter 3.
5. John Heneage Jesse, *Memoirs of the Court of England ... from 1688 to the death of George II* (London, 1843), vol. 3, p. 8.
6. 'I have not one drop of blood in my veins which isn't English': George Augustus, c.1714–15, ibid., vol. 3, p. 4.
7. See A. and H. Tayler, *1715: The Story of the Rising* (London: Nelson, 1936).
8. Thompson, *George II*, p. 48.
9. Colin Haydon, 'The Fifteen and its Aftermath', in *Anti-Catholicism in Eighteenth Century England, c.1714–80: A Political and Social Study* (Manchester: Manchester University Press, 1993), chapter 3; Susannah Abbott, 'Clerical responses to the Jacobite Rebellion in 1715', *Historical Research*, vol. 76 (193, 2003), pp. 332–46.
10. Even so, the 'Exercise of Healing', designed to accompany the ritual of the Royal Touch for the cure of scrofula, remained in the *Book of Common Prayer*. See Stephen Brogan, *The Royal Touch in Early Modern England: Politics, Medicine and Sin* (Martlesham: Boydell & Brewer, 2015).

11. The custom of public dining belonged to the trappings of absolutism, and would apparently be taken up by George Augustus at Herrenhausen after he became king-elector. See Bernd Adam, 'Herrenhausen: The Historical Summer Residence of the Welfs', in *Schloss Herrenhausen* (Munich: Hirmer, 2013), p. 25.

12. Dr Lucy Worsley sympathizes more with George Augustus's personality than with his Electorate. See 'Why do the Georgians matter?', *BBC Magazine* (May 2014), www.lucy-worsley.com/why-do-the-georgians-matter (2019).

13. The king-elector consulted a group of twelve judges on the question of whether English law would permit him to deprive George Augustus permanently of his paternal rights. The judges' opinion was negative, but the episode convinced Princess Caroline that her husband's low opinion of his father was well justified. The prince then sought remedy at law to regain immediate custody of his children, but without success. See Jesse, *Memoirs of the Court of England*, vol. 3, p. 6.

14. Sung to the tune of 'Chevy Chase', and quoted by Lucy Worsley, *Courtiers: The Secret History of the Georgian Court* (London: Faber & Faber, 2010), p. 35.

15. Leicester House was built in 1635 by Robert Sydney, 2nd Earl of Leicester, on land to the north of Leicester Fields, in the area of Westminster now known as Leicester Square, WC2. Very appropriately, sixty years previously it had been the last residence of Elizabeth Stuart, ex-Queen of Bohemia, George Augustus's great-grandmother. It was demolished c.1791.

16. See J. Van der Kiste, *King George II and Queen Caroline* (Stroud: Sutton, 1997).

17. After Walpole's death, a substantial number of his pictures were bought by an art dealer in Berlin, who sold them on in 1764 to the Empress Catherine. See Geraldine Norman, *The Hermitage: The Biography of a Great Museum* (New York: Fromm, 1998).

18. Robert Walpole's nickname was 'Robin', hence 'Robinocracy'.

19. See J. H. Plumb, *Sir Robert Walpole: The Making of a Statesman* (London: Allen Lane, 1972).

20. Usually translated as 'Let sleeping dogs lie', and first recorded in the Memoirs of Walpole's son, Horace; the modern equivalent is 'If it ain't broke, don't fix it.'

21. See Vanessa Berridge, *The Princess's Garden: Royal Intrigues and the Untold Story of Kew* (Stroud: Amberley, 2015), chapter 1.

22. The twin duchies of Bremen and Verden (but not the city of Bremen) were captured from Sweden by Danish forces in 1712 then sold to Brunswick-Lüneburg for one million riks-dollars and eventually confirmed in 1733 as an imperial fief (see map). See H.-E. Dannenberg and H.-J. Schulze, *Geschichte des Landes zwischen Elbe und Weser* (Hamburg: Landschaftsverband, 1995–2008, 3 vols).

23. See Jeremy Black, *Politics and Foreign Policy in the Age of George I* (Farnham: Ashgate, 2014).

24. See Ragnhild Hatton, *Charles XII of Sweden* (London: Historical Association, 1974).

25. The unmarried Charles XII was succeeded by his sister, Ulrika Eleanora, who abdicated in 1720 in favour of her husband, Frederick of Hesse-Kassel. Ten years later, the Swedish monarch succeeded his father as *Landgraf* of Hesse-Kassel, creating the composite state of Sweden-Finland-Hesse-Kassel, which lasted until his death in 1751.

26. John Chamberlayne, *Magnae Britanniae Notitia, or The Present State of Great Britain, with diverse remarks about the Antient State Thereof, 27th Edition* (London, 1726), book 2, pp. 45–6. The first edition had been published by Chamberlayne's father Edward in 1708 following the Act of Union. The book, whose later editions followed a Hanoverian or 'loyalist' interpretation of many constitutional issues, continued to be regularly revised and re-published until 1755.

27. Ibid., book 1, part 1, chapter 2, 'Of the King of England', p. 45.

4. 1727–1760: ON THE THRONE, PART I – COURTIERS, CLERICS, SIXPENCE AND SLAVES

1. heraldica.org/topics/Britain/brit-proclamations.htm#George2 (21 June 2016).
2. Erected in 1751 in St Helier's Vier Marchi or Old Market, the statue sculpted by John Cheere marks a gift of £200 from the king-elector for the construction of the town's harbour, <tripadvisor.co.uk/Attraction_Review_g551613_d17630797_Reviews-George_II_Statue> (2020).
3. *A Foreign View of England in the reigns of George I and George II: The Letters of César de Saussure to his family* (trans. and ed. Mme Van Muyden) (London: John Murray, 1902), letter IX, p. 239 ff.
4. The Dymoke family were hereditary champions, <historicengland.org.uk>listing>the-list>list-entry>Scrivelsby-Court> (2020).
5. <bbc.co.uk/teach/ten-pieces/KS2-george-friderik-handel-zadok-the-priest/znvrkmn> (2020).
6. Heinrich Dittmer, *Authentische und vollständing Beschreiben aller Feyerlichkeiten . . . im dem Hanoverschen Lande . . .* (Hanover, 1822), p. 49 ff.
7. Royal Standard, 1714–1837, /<en.wikipedia.org/wiki/Royal_coat_of_arms_of_the_United_Kingdom#After_the_Acts_of_Union_1707> (2020).
8. Wendland, <en.wikibedia.ru>wiki>Hanoverian_Wendland> (2020).
9. *Memoirs of Charles-Lewis, Baron von Pollnitz* (London, 1738, 3 vols), vol. 3 on 'Wolfembuttel', pp. 114–19, on 'Brunswic, Zell and Hanover', pp. 119–23.
10. See Matthew Jeffries, *Hamburg: A Cultural and Literary History* (Oxford: Signal Books, 2011).
11. Sandstein Museum, Bad Bentheim, <mindat.org/loc-286124.html> (2020).
12. See Linda Colley, *Britons: Forging the Nation, 1707–1837* (New Haven, CT and London: Yale University Press, 2008); Colley argues that 'the early Georgians failed to take the opportunities of stressing Britishness', and that a strong sense of Britishness only emerged in the later eighteenth century.
13. See James Curl, *Georgian Architecture* (Newton Abbot: David & Charles, 1993).
14. See Anne Kershen, *Strangers, Aliens and Asians: Huguenots, Jews and Bangladeshis in Spitalfields, 1600–2000* (London: Routledge, 2005).
15. Claude Aymand was credited with performing the world's first successful appendicitis operation; see W. J. Bishop, *The Early History of Surgery* (London: Robert Hale, 1960).
16. See Alan Swanson, *David Garrick and the Development of English Comedy* (London: Edwin Mellen Press, 2013).
17. See Philip Phillips and W. Hanneford-Smith, *Paul de Lamerie, Citizen and Goldsmith: A Study of his Work 1688–1751* (London: Holland Press, 1968).
18. See Abel Boyer, *The Royal Dictionary, French and English, English and French* (London, 1729), with an Introduction by Queen Caroline. This dictionary, the first of its kind, ran into dozens of editions between 1699 and 1765.
19. See John Summerson, *Georgian London* (London: Penguin, 1991).
20. See R. J. Minney, *No. 10 Downing Street: A House in History* (London: Cassell, 1963).
21. Newfoundland (1583), Virginia (1609), Bermuda (1615), Barbados (1621), Barbuda (1628), Massachusetts (1629), Antigua (1632), Maryland (1632), Connecticut (1636), Bay Islands (1643), Bahamas (1648), Jamaica (1660), Carolina (1663), Rhode Island

(1663), New Jersey (1664), Delaware (1664), St Lucia (1667), Leeward Islands (1671), New Hampshire (1679), Pennsylvania (1681), New York (1685), Gibraltar (1704), St Kitts (1713), Nova Scotia (1713) and Minorca (1708–13). Under George Augustus, Carolina was split into North and South Carolina in 1729, and Georgia founded in 1732. Minorca was lost in 1756.

22. See K. Coleman (ed.), *A History of Georgia* (Athens, GA: University of Georgia Press, 1991).

23. *Encyclopaedia Britannica* (11th edn, 1912), vol. 11, pp. 755–7.

24. Lucy Worsley, *Courtiers*, p. 3 ff.

25. St James's Palace, as described in 1740 by the Prussian Baron Bielefeld: Bielefeld's 'Letters', *Literary Review*, vol. 42 (1770), p. 274 ff.

26. Worsley, *Courtiers*, p. 11.

27. Ibid.

28. Ibid.

29. Ibid.

30. Ibid.

31. See Elias Ashmole, *The Institution, Laws and Ceremonies of the most Noble Order of the Garter* (London, 1693).

32. See Peter Galloway, *The Order of the Thistle* (London: Spink & Son, 2009).

33. Peter Vansittart, *Orders of Chivalry* (London: Bodley Head, 1958).

34. See A. Hanham, 'Charles FitzRoy, second Duke of Grafton', *Oxford Dictionary of National Biography* (Oxford: Oxford University Press, 2007).

35. See Dominic Shellard (ed.), *The Lord Chamberlain Regrets: A History of British Theatre Censorship* (London: British Library, 2004). The Examiner of Plays and his deputy answered to the Lord Chamberlain.

36. Nigel Aston, 'The Court of George II: Lord Berkeley of Stratton's perspective', *Court Historian*, XIII (2008), pp. 171–93.

37. See the Database of Court Officers (DCO), <courtofficers.ctsdh.luc.edu> (2020).

38. See J. Dunford, *History of the Sardinian Chapel* (London: R. & T. Washbourne, 1905).

39. In 1729, during the reign of the childless and pro-Spanish Antonio Farnese, the duchy of Parma was occupied by Spanish troops, thereby offending both the Empire and Great Britain.

40. See R. Williams, *Rousham* (Oxford, 1996); C. Hussey, *A Georgian Arcady: William Kent's Gardens at Rousham* (Oxford, 1946); Samuel Baker, *A Catalogue of the Genuine and Elegant Library of the late Sir Clement Cottrell Dormer . . .* (London, 1764).

41. A vampire scare swept Germany in the 1720s, launching the so-called 'Vampire Controversy'; see M. J. Trow, *A Brief History of Vampires* (London: Robinson, 2010). The king-elector quarrelled on the subject with Walpole, who called vampires 'imaginary blood-suckers', Jesse, *Memoirs of the Court of England*, vol. 3, p. 32.

42. On Voltaire see René Pomeau, *Voltaire en son temps* (Paris: Fayard, 1995).

43. See Eric Gritsch, *A History of Lutheranism* (Minneapolis, MN: Fortress Press, 2010).

44. www.tripadvisor.co.uk >Tourism-g187352–Hildesheim> (2019).

45. See Eric Beyreuther, *Geschichte des Pietismus* (Stuttgart: Steinkopf, 1978).

46. See Francis Yarker, *The Vicar of Bray* (London: Excalibur Press, 1993). It is uncertain whether the good vicar officiated at Bray in Berkshire or Bray in County Wicklow.

47. See David Hemptron, *Methodism: The Empire of the Spirit* (New Haven, CT and London: Yale University Press, 2005).

48. Chamberlayne, *Magnae Britanniae Notitia*, book 2, p. 44.

49. The Bangorian Controversy, named after Benjamin Hoadly, then Bishop of Bangor, was a bitterly fought theological debate over the nature of Church authority which led to the

long-term suspension of Convocation. See Andrew Starkie, *The Church of England and the Bangorian Controversy, 1716–21* (Woodbridge: Boydell Press, 2007).

50. Horace Walpole, *The Letters of Horace Walpole, Earl of Orford* (London, 1840, 6 vols), vol. 4, *passim*.

51. See Daniel Neal, *The History of the Puritans and Non-conformists* (London, 1754).

52. David S. Katz, *The Jews in the History of England, 1485–1850* (Oxford: Clarendon Press, 1994), p. 267 ff.; see also Saul Friedman, *Jews and the American Slave Trade* (New Brunswick, NJ: Transaction Publishers, 1998).

53. Johnson Grant, *A Summary of the History of the English Church* (London, 1820), vol. 3, pp. 167–8.

54. Selina Hastings and Elizabeth Einberg, 'Elegant Revolutionaries', in *Ladies of Quality and Distinction Catalogue* (London: Foundling Hospital, 2018).

55. See Eamon Duffy (ed.), *Challoner and his Church: A Catholic Bishop in Georgian England* (London: Darton, Longman & Todd, 1981).

56. See William Gibson, *Enlightenment Prelate: Benjamin Hoadly* (Cambridge: James Clarke, 2004).

57. 'The public Arianism of William Whiston', in Maurice Wiles, *Archetypal Heresy: Arianism Through the Centuries* (Oxford: Clarendon Press, 1996).

58. Johnson Grant, *Summary of the History of the English Church and of the sects which have departed from its communion* (London, 1825), chapter 18, 'The Reign of George II'.

59. Quoted by Wiles, *Archtypal Heresy*, *passim*.

60. See Gould, Robert Freke, *The Concise History of Freemasonry* (London: Gale & Polden, 1920).

61. See John Coustos, *The Suffering of John Coustos, for Free-masonry and for his refusing to turn Roman Catholic* (Dublin, 1746).

62. M. de Voltaire, *Letters Concerning the English Nation* (London, 1733), p. 30.

63. M. Thornton, 'Richard Cantillon', <mises.org/profile/Richard-cantillon> 2020.

64. Both Bielfeld and Achenwall used statistical methods to describe the political economy of contemporary countries: See Jakub Bielfeld, *Institutions Politiques* (1770); Gottfried Achenwall, *Grundsätze der Europäischen Geschichte* (1754), with later editions.

65. Selma Stern, *The Court Jew: A Contribution to the History of Absolutism in Europe* (London: Routledge, 1950).

66. Linda Frey, 'Charles Townsend, 2nd Viscount Townsend', *Oxford Dictionary of National Biography* (Oxford: Oxford University Press, 2004).

67. See Mark Overton, *Agricultural Revolution in England: The Transformation of the Agrarian Economy 1500–1850* (Cambridge: Cambridge University Press, 1996).

68. See Christian Stenglin, *The Hanoverian* (London: J. A. Allen, 1990).

69. From Oliver Goldsmith, 'The Deserted Village' (1770), <poetryfoundation.rg/poems/44292/the-deserted-village> (2020).

70. John Nichols, *Literary Anecdotes of the Eighteenth Century, Additions to the Sixth Volume* (London, 1815), vol. 9, p. 642.

71. <en.numista.com> (2020).

72. www.coindatabase.com (2020). Inscriptions varied, but the magnificent gold guinea of 1758 bore the king-elector's titles in full: M+B+F+ET+H+REX FD B+L+D S+R+I+A+T+ET+E. See <royalmint.com/our-coins/ ranges/historic-coins/historic-guineas/george-II-gold-guinea> (2020). From 1725, the Bank of England issued half-printed paper banknotes, at first in a £50 denomination, and from 1748 in denominations up to £1,000. See Katie Allen, 'Banknotes: a short history', the *Guardian*, 10 September 2013. The average family income was £25–£30 per annum.

73. 'Regal Irish Coppers', <coins.nd.edu/ColCoin/ColCoinText/Br-IrishCopper.2.html> (2020).

74. The origins of this nursery rhyme are hotly disputed, and some lines and phrases seem to go back to the sixteenth century. The text of 1744 appears to have built on the earlier versions. <allnurseryrhymes.com/sing-a-song-of-sixpence> (2020).

75. In addition, the house of Orange from the United Provinces had supplied a King of England – William III (r. 1689–1702), and the house of Brunswick-Wolfenbüttel was homing in on the throne of Russia (see Chapter 7).

76. See Eda Sagarra, A Social History of Germany, 1648–1914 (London: Transaction Publishers, 2003).

77. See J. Rogalla von Bieberstein, Adelsherrschaft und Adelskultur in Deutschland (Limburg: C. A. Starke, 1998).

78. <en.wikipedia.org/wiki/German_Timber_Frame_Road> (2019).

79. 'Goettingen Stadt Home', <goettingen.de/index.php?lang=en> (2020).

80. See Charles White, A Compendium of the British Peerage (London, 1825).

81. See R. Browning, The Duke of Newcastle (New Haven, CT and London: Yale University Press, 1975).

82. See Lewis Namier, The Structure of Politics at the Accession of George III (London: Macmillan, 1929).

83. The king-elector's first appointment after his coronation in October 1727 was to attend the Lord Mayor's parade and banquet, and he continued to make regular appearances in public – at military parades, at Maundy Thursday ceremonies in the 1730s and at royal birthday celebrations. See M. C. Kilburn, 'Royalty and the Public in Britain, 1714–89', Oxford DPhil thesis, 1997, chapter 2, 'Loud and Repeated Huzzas', and chapter 3, 'Royal Appearances in Public'.

84. See Peter Straub, The Hellfire Club (London: HarperCollins, 1997). Dashwood, who held a minor post in the court of Frederick, Prince of Wales, was an associate of other profligates like Bubb Dodington and John Montague, Earl of Sandwich (1718–92) – eponymous inventor of the sandwich – but also contrived to be an active MP, a FRS, a DCL (Oxon.) and Chancellor of the Exchequer (1762–3). See Betty Kemp, Sir Francis Dashwood: An Eighteenth-Century Independent (New York: St Martin's Press, 1967).

85. Harris's List of Covent-Garden Ladies or Man of Pleasures's Kalender for the Year 1789 [and] many preceding years (London, 1757–89), pp. 17–18.

86. T. H. White, The Age of Scandal: An Excursion into a Minor Period (London: Jonathan Cape, 1950), p. 155.

87. See Alysa Levene, Childcare, Health and Mortality in the London Foundling Hospital, 1741–1800 (Manchester: Manchester University Press, 2007).

88. See 'Transatlantic Slave Trade', <liverpoolmuseums.org.uk/transatlantic-slave-trade> (2020); Anthony Tibbles, Liverpool and the Slave Trade (Liverpool: Liverpool University Press, 2018).

89. See Herbert S. Klein, The Atlantic Slave Trade (Cambridge: Cambridge University Press, 2010); Jeremy Black, The Atlantic Slave Trade in World History (London: Routledge, 2015); Marcus Rediger, The Slave Ship: A Human History (London: John Murray, 2007).

90. For John Newton see Jonathan Aitken, John Newton: From Disgrace to Amazing Grace (London: Continuum, 2007), also Newton's Journal of a Slave-Trader, 1750–54 (London: Epworth Press, 1962). His Olney Hymns (London, 1779) contains 'Glorious Things of Thee are Spoken', 'How Sweet the Name of Jesus Sounds' and 'Amazing Grace'.

91. Natalie Zenon Davies, quoted by Leo d'Anjou, Social Movements and Cultural Change: The First Abolition Campaign Revisited (New York: de Gruyter, 1996), p. 118.

5. HEAD OF THE FAMILY FIRM

1. Sophia Dorothea of Celle died at Schloss Ahlden on Lüneburger Heath in November 1726, leaving memoirs published long after her death. See *The Memoirs of Sophie Dorothea, Consort of George I* (London, 1846, 2 vols).

2. General George Howe (1725–58) killed at Ticonderoga, Admiral Richard Howe (1726–99), and General Sir William Howe (1729–1814). See Ira Gruber, *The Howe Brothers and the American Revolution* (Chapel Hill, NC: University of North Carolina Press, 1975).

3. Quoted by Chenevix-Trench, *George II*, p. 155.

4. From Lord Hervey, *Memoirs of the Court of George II* (London, 1848).

5. Contradictory evidence surrounds George Augustus's attitude to child-rearing. His crapulous reaction to the Duchess of Marlborough when she tried to console one of his crying children may not be entirely typical: 'The trouble with you English', he said, 'is that you are never whipped when young.' (See Jesse, *Memoirs of the Court of England*, vol. 3, p. 44.) Yet the physical chastisement of children was as common in England as in Germany, and in later life George Augustus expressed regret. 'I did not love my children when they were young,' he admitted in 1751, 'but now I love them as most fathers.' (Thompson, *George II*, p. 213).

6. Lord Waldegrave, quoted by Jesse, *Memoirs of the Court of England*, vol. 3, p. 25.

7. Jasmeet Barker, 'Fiddles and Dancing at George II's Court', <blog.hrp.org.uk/curators/fiddles-dancing-at-George-iis-court> (2020).

8. Jesse, *Memoirs of the Court of England*, vol. 3, p. 5.

9. <historyhome.co.uk/people/george2.htm> (2020).

10. Alexander Pope, 'On a certain lady at Court', www.poemhunter.com>poem>on-a-certain-lady-at-court> (2017).

11. Quoted by Lucy Worsley, *Courtiers*, pp. 270–71.

12. Bubb Dodington, Lord Melcombe, was independently wealthy and always closely associated with Frederick, Prince of Wales, on whose behalf he may have been a 'spy-master'. See John Carswell, 'George Bubb Dodington', *History Today*, vol. 4, 12 December 1954; also Lewis Lesley, *Connoisseurs and Secret Agents in Eighteenth-Century Rome* (London: Chatto & Windus, 1961).

13. The marriage scheme was finally scotched in the summer of 1730 by the failure of the mission to Berlin of Charles Hotham. See Thompson, *George II*, pp. 82–4.

14. See John Walter, *The Royal Griffin: Frederick, Prince of Wales, 1707–51* (London: Jarrolds, 1972); Kimberley Rorschauch, 'Frederick, Prince of Wales as collector and patron', *Walpole Society Volumes*, vol. 55 (1989–90), pp. 1–76.

15. Natasha Lavender, 'These British monarchs had the weirdest food habits', 15 July 2014, <soyummy.com/strange_british_royal_food_habits> (2020). Two menus were sold at auction in London in 2014. The mention of songbirds accords with the first verse of 'Sing a song of sixpence', where 'four and twenty blackbirds [are] baked in a pie' (see above).

16. See Aileen Ribeiro, *Dress in Eighteenth Century Europe, 1715–1789* (New Haven, CT and London: Yale University Press, 2002).

17. 10 September 1737, George II to Prince Frederick. Published for the Georgian Papers Programme and officially described as a copy of the original, though surely a translation. https://www.aol.co.uk/news/2017/12/06/online-king-george-ii-letter

18. Johann Ludwig Wallmoden-Gimborn, <en.wikipedia.org/wiki/House_of_Wallmoden> (2020).

19. From *The Bielfeld Letters* (London, 1768–70), quoted by Thompson, *George II*, p. 136.
20. See Basil Williams, *Carteret and Newcastle: A Contrast in Contemporaries* (1943; Cambridge: Cambridge University Press, 2014).
21. From Lord John Hervey, *Memoirs of the Court of George II* (London, 1848), *passim*.
22. Edgar Shepherd, *Memorials of St James's Palace* (London, 1894), vol. 1, p. 86, after Horace Walpole.
23. See Brendan Simms, *Three Victories and a Defeat: The Rise and Fall of the First British Empire, 1714–83* (London: Penguin, 2007). Simms argues that the Europe-centred policy of the early Georgian period kept Britain safe, whereas the isolationist line of George III led to disaster and the loss of the American colonies.
24. Samuel Johnson, 'London: A poem in imitation of the Third Satire of Juvenal' (London, 1738), lines 49–56.
25. 'Rule Britannia' <historic-uk.com/HistoryUK/HistoryofBritain/Rule-Britannia> (2020).
26. Augusta (1737–1813), eldest daughter of Frederick, Prince Wales, married in 1764 to the Duke of Brunswick-Wolfenbüttel and mother of the future Queen Caroline of Brunswick.
27. See Edward Pearce, *Pitt the Elder: Man of War* (London: Bodley Head, 2010), p. 274.
28. First published anonymously in *Thesaurus Musicus* (1744), where the new lyrics were combined with a much older melody. See J. Stevenson, *God Save the King! The National Anthem of England* (London, 1830).
29. Quoted by Rebecca Starr Brown, <RBS.com/2018/91/11/George-ii-caroline-of-ansbachs-hatred-for-their-eldest-son> (2019).
30. The full text reads: 'Here lies poor Fred / Who was alive but is dead. / Had it been his father / I would have rather. / Had it been his brother, / Better than another. / Had it been his sister / No one would have missed her. / Had it been the whole generation, / So much better for the nation. / But since 'tis only Fred / Who was alive and is dead, / There's no more to be said.' Variously described as 'anonymous' and a 'Jacobite song', it was quoted by Thackeray, *The Four Georges*. See Richard Cavendish, 'The Death of Frederick, Prince of Wales', *History Today*, vol. 51(3), March 2001.
31. Royal Archives, GEO/MAIN/52955–6. Quoted in 'Preview of the Papers of George II', <rct.uk/collection/Georgian-papers-programme/George-ii> (2020).
32. Ibid. GEO/MAIN/52967, 5 May 1757.
33. T. H. White, *The Age of Scandal: An Excursion through a Minor Period* (London: Cape, 1950).

6. GEORGE AUGUSTUS: A POLITICAL ANIMAL

1. Chenevix-Trench, *George II*, p. 155.
2. The obvious example is Charles XI of Sweden, who formally declared his government to be absolute in 1670. The Oldenburgs of Denmark followed the same tradition.
3. Thompson, *George II*, p. 9.
4. 'Privy Council of Hanover', https://en.wikipedia.org/wiki/Privy_Council_of_Hanover (2019).
5. G. H. Guttridge, *The Early Career of Lord Rockingham, 1730–64* (Berkeley: University of California, 1952).
6. <en.wikipedia.org/Oaths_of_ Allegiance> (2019). Oaths of Abjuration originated from the Security of the Succession Act, 1702.
7. Walpole, *Memoirs*, p. 178.

8. Ibid., p. 180.

9. Jesse, *Memoirs of the Court of England*, vol. 3, p. 27. Walpole, who had suffered years of abuse from the 'Patriots', was blamed for the Anglo-Spanish War, and performed poorly in the general election of 1741.

10. Ibid., p. 22.

11. James, 3rd Earl of Berkeley, PC (1679–1736), sometime First Lord of the Admiralty and a royal favourite, had been suspected during the family fracas of 1717 of preparing a plan to have George Augustus deported to America. He was dismissed before the coronation of 1727 and died in France. Jesse, *Memoirs of the Court of England*, vol. 3, p. 10.

12. Minority of the Successor to the Crown Act, 1751. See Walpole, *Memoirs*, p. 165.

13. Jesse, *Memoirs of the Court of England*, vol. 3, p. 40.

14. Chamberlayne, *Magnae Britanniae Notitia*, book 2, p. 45.

15. Benjamin Bühring, 'The German Chancery in London', in *Als die Royals aus Hannover Kamen* (Hanover: Sandstein, 2014), pp. 106–15.

16. Ibid. Several of the king-elector's best cryptoanalists, such as Bode, Lampe and Neuburg, were recruited from the electoral service. See David Kahn, *The Codebreakers: The Comprehensive History of Secret Communication* (1967; New York: Scribner, 1996), chapter 5, 'The Era of the Black Chambers'.

17. See Kahn, *The Codebreakers*, also Christopher Andrew, *The Secret World: A History of Intelligence* (London: Penguin, 2018).

18. Address by the Lords to King George II on the Opening of Parliament, 16 February 1738, 'As reported 280 years ago', *Belfast Newsletter Online*, 16 February 2019.

19. 'The King's Speeches at opening the first session', First Parliament of George II, begins 23 January 1728, *British History Online*.

20. John Almon, *A Review of the Reign of George II* (London, 1762), p. 32.

21. See R. J. Robson, *The Oxfordshire Election of 1754: A Study in the Interplay of City, County and University Politics* (Oxford: Oxford University Press, 1949).

22. Xavier Cervantes, 'L'image du souverain dans les opéras londiniens de Haendel: réalité et representation'; Joel Richard, 'Le *Solomon* (1747) de Haendel: le souverain en majesté', in Marie-Claire Rouyer, *Figures du Souverain* (Bordeaux: Université Michel de Montaigne, 1996), p. 84 ff.

23. *London Gazette* no. 7567 (11–14 December 1736), no. 7569 (18–21 December 1736), no. 7571 (25–8 December 1736) and no. 7576 (11–15 January 1736).

24. Jesse, *Memoirs of the Court of England*, vol. 3, p. 31.

25. Brendan McConville, discussing 'the cult of monarchy' in colonial America 'in print and pulpit', attributes the king-elector's high reputation to his longevity, to stable economic growth and to dislike for the Jacobites, concluding that 'it is hard to overstate [George Augustus's] popularity in British America', in Andreas Gestrich and Michael Schaich (eds), *The Hanoverian Succession: Dynastic Politics and Monarchical Culture* (Abingdon: Routledge, 2016), p. 177 ff.

7. ON THE THRONE, PART II – POETS, PARDONS AND PREROGATIVES

1. 'boets and bainters', see https://britroyals.com/kings.asp?id=george2; https://en-wikiquote.org.wiki/George_II_of_Great_Britain (2019). J. Ireland and J. Nichols, *Hogarth's Works* (London, 1883), p. 122.

2. See James Prior, *The Life of Edward Malone* (London, 1860), p. 369.

3. See Jane Glover, *Handel in London: The Making of a Genius* (London: Macmillan, 2018).

4. Probably another confabulation.

5. Tenor aria from Handel's opera *Semele* (1744), <genius.com/George-frideric-handel-whereer-you-walk-lyrics> (2017).

6. <classicfm.com/composers/Stanley/music/john-stanley-trumpet-voluntary> (2020).

7. www.allmusic.com>william-boyce-mn0001162453> (2020).

8. Colley Cibber, C., *An Apology for the Life of Colley Cibber* (1740; London, 1889).

9. Cibber, 'The Blind Boy', https://www.poemhunter.com/poem/the-blind-boy-#content (2019).

10. See Helene Coon, *Colley Cibber: A Biography* (Lexington, KY: University Press of Kentucky, 1986).

11. Educational institutions came within the purview of the state Church. See www.topuniversities.comuniversity-gottingen> (2018).

12. See Don Oberdorfer, *Princeton University: The First 250 Years* (Princeton, NJ: Trustees of Princeton University, 1995).

13. See Robert A. McCaughey, *Stand, Columbia: A History of Columbia University in the City of New York, 1754-2004* (New York: Columbia University Press, 2003).

14. Loyalist professors from King's College, New York, migrated to Nova Scotia during the Revolutionary War. See Stephen Poole, *Halifax: Discovering Its Heritage* (Halifax, NS: Formac, 2012).

15. See Giles Mandelbrote and Barry Taylor, *Libraries Within the Library: The Origins of the British Library's Printed Collections* (London: British Library, 2009).

16. Roger Emerson, 'The World in which the Scottish Enlightenment took shape', in Aaron Garrett and James A. Harris, *Scottish Philosophy in the Eighteenth Century*, vol. 1: *Morals, Politics, Art, Religion* (Oxford: Oxford University Press, 2015), chapter 1.

17. <en.wikipedia.org/wiki/List_of_fellows_of_the_Royal_Society_elected_in_1727> (2020).

18. See Joan Evans, *A History of the Society of Antiquaries* (Oxford: Oxford University Press, 1956).

19. See Jane Brown, *The Omnipotent Magician: Lancelot 'Capability' Brown 1716-1783* (London: Chatto & Windus, 2011).

20. 'Stowe House: Discover the Hidden Secrets Inside', 'Stowe House: Gardens and Parkland' (National Trust, Stowe, 2016).

21. See Peter Quennell, *Hogarth's Progress* (London: Collins, 1955).

22. Henry Carey, 'A poem to His Majesty, George II, in Liliputian Verse . . .' (1727), reprinted in *Poems on Several Occasions, by Henry Carey* (London, 1729). <writersinspire.org/content/poem-his-majesty-george-ii-present-state-of-affairs> (2019).

23. <Westminster-abbey,org/abbey-commemorations/commemorations/john-gay> (2020).

24. Alexander Pope, *The Dunciad*, book 4 (London, 1743), lines 181-8.

25. Johnson, from *Letter to Lord Chesterfield*. See W. Jackson Bate, *Samuel Johnson: A Biography* (London: Chatto & Windus, 1978).

26. Samuel Johnson, *A Dictionary of the English Language* (Dublin, 1768).

27. Carol Flynn, 'Samuel Richardson', in Robert L. Caserio and Clement Hawes (eds), *The Cambridge History of the English Novel* (Cambridge: Cambridge University Press, 2012), pp. 97-112.

28. See Sarah Fielding, *The Governess; or, Little Female Academy* (1749; Peterborough, Ont.: Broadview Press, 2005).

29. Henry Fielding's *The History of Tom Jones, a Foundling* (London, 2 vols), was inspired by the Foundling Hospital.

30. See J. M. Beattie, *The First English Detectives: The Bow Street Runners* (Oxford: Oxford University Press, 2012).

31. 'Old England's Roast Beef', first heard in Fielding's *Grub Street Opera* (1731).

32. Chamberlayne *Magnae Britanniae Notitia*, book 2, p. 45.

33. The Proceedings in Courts of Justice Act, 1730 (4 Geo II c 26) also applied to the Court of the Exchequer in Scotland.

34. 'The Bloody Code', <en.wikipedia.org/wiki/Capital_punishment_in_the_United_Kingdom> (2019).

35. 1751 Murder Act (25 Geo II c 37), <en.wikisource.org/wiki/<Murder_Act_1751> (2017), also known, due to the change of the calendar that year, as 'The Murder Act, 1752'.

36. 1777, on the execution of the Revd William Dodds, <britishexecutions.co.uk/execution-/content=William%20Dodds> (2020).

37. <constitution.org/primarysources/blackstone.html> (2020).

38. Portal: Acts of the Parliament of the United Kingdom/ George II (wikisource) (2020).

39. Chamberlayne, *Magnae Britanniae Notitia*, book 2, pp. 45–6.

40. The Great Seal, <en.wikipedia.org.wiki/Great_Seal_of_the_Realm#Union_of_the_Crowns> (2020).

41. Paul Wells, hanged in Oxford, had been convicted of changing one digit in a date from '2' to '3' in a letter to Elizabeth Croke, to whom he owed a small sum of money. See <britishexecutions.co.uk> (2020).

42. J. S. Puetter <de.wikipedia.org>wiki>Johann_Stefan_Puetter> (2020).

43. See George Harris, *The Life of Lord Chancellor Hardwicke* (London, 1847, 3 vols).

44. See Cecil Fifoote, *Lord Mansfield* (Oxford: Clarendon Press, 1936).

45. In 1729, Sir Philip Yorke, then Attorney General, co-issued the Yorke-Talbot Opinion, which upheld the legality of slavery in England and which was later overturned by Lord Mansfield's ruling in the Somerset Case of 1772, <en.wikipedia.org>wiki>Yorke-Talbot_slavery_opinion> (2020). David Allen Green, 'Why lawyers were as culpable as any slavers', *Prospect Magazine*, 10 July 2020.

46. See Wilfrid Prest, *William Blackstone: Law and Letters in the Eighteenth Century* (Oxford: Oxford University Press, 2008).

47. See Montesquieu, *De l'Esprit des lois*, published as *The Spirit of Laws, translated from the French* (London, 1750).

48. Ursula Gonthier, *Montesquieu and England: Enlightened Exchanges, 1689–1755* (Abingdon: Routledge, 2016), p. 52 ff.

49. 'The Hanover Army', <spanishsuccession.nl/hanover_army.htlm> (2017); 'Hanoverian Army', from the Seven Years War Project, <kronoskaf.com/syw/indexphp?=Hanoverian Army> (2020).

50. Spoerken led the Hanoverian contingent at Minden. See <rct.uk/collection/402745/general-feldmarschall-von-sporken> (2020).

51. See N. A. M. Rodger, *The Command of the Ocean: A Naval History of Britain 1649–1815* (London: Penguin, 2006).

52. See David Hannay, *A Short History of the Royal Navy* (London: Methuen, 1898, 2 vols).

53. W. A. Anson, *The Life of Admiral Lord Anson, the Father of the British Navy, 1697–1762* (London: John Murray, 1912).

54. Jesse, *Memoirs of the Court of England*, vol. 3, p. 27.

55. 'Origins of Trooping the Colour', www.householddivision.org.uk (2020).

56. Lt-Gen. Humphrey Bland, *A Treatise of Military Discipline* (London, 1727).

57. Royal Artillery <army.mod.uk/who-we-are/corps-regiments-and-units/royal-artillery> (2020).

58. See David G. Chandler and I. F. W. Beckett, *The Oxford History of the British Army* (Oxford: Oxford University Press, 2003).

59. <contemplator.com/tunebook/England.grenadr.htm> (2020).

60. Reviewed in 1728 by the king-elector on Blackheath.

61. A. Massie, 'Manners, John, Marquis of Granby, 1721–70', *Oxford Dictionary of National Biography*, https://doi.org/10.1093/ref:odnb/17958 (2019)

62. See W. S. Churchill, *Marlborough: His Life and Times* (Chicago: University of Chicago Press, 2002, 4 vols).

63. Jeremy Black, *British Diplomats and Diplomacy, 1688–1800* (Exeter: University of Exeter Press, 2001) p. 28 ff; also his 'Hanover and British foreign policy, 1714–60', *English Historical Review*, 120(486) (2005), pp. 303–39; U. Dann, *Hannover und England, 1740–60: Diplomatie und Selbsterhaltung* (Hildesheim: August Lax, 1986).

64. Widely quoted without attribution. See Francis Parkman, *Montcalm and Wolfe* (Boston, 1884), p. 113.

65. See Charles Petrie, *Diplomatic History 1713–1933* (London: Hollis & Carter, 1946).

66. See D. B. Horn, *Sir Charles Hanbury Williams and European Diplomacy* (London: Harrap, 1930).

67. *The Odes of Sir Charles Hanbury Williams* (Farmington Hills, MI: Gale, 2010), p. 129.

68. <best-quotations.com/authquotes.php?auth=159> (2019).

69. Almon, *Review*, p. 83.

70. See David Armitage, *Ideological Origins of the British Empire* (Cambridge: Cambridge University Press, 2000); Brendan Simms, *Three Victories and a Defeat: The Rise and Fall of the First British Empire* (London: Penguin, 2007).

71. See Max Savelle, *Empires to Nations: Expansion in America, 1713–1824* (Minneapolis, MN: University of Minnesota Press, 1976).

72. See J. L. Sutton, *The King's Honor and the King's Cardinal: The War of the Polish Succession* (Lexington, KY: University Press of Kentucky, 1980).

73. <historic-uk.com/HistoryUK/HistoryofEngland/War-of-Jenkins-Ear > (2019).

74. See M. S. Anderson, *The War of Austrian Succession, 1740–1748* (London: Longman, 1995); Reed Browning, *The War of the Austrian Succession* (London: Palgrave Macmillan, 1993).

75. Jesse, *Memoirs of the Court of England*, vol. 3, pp. 44–5.

76. Pitt quote, 10 December 1742, <en.wikisource.org/wiki/Dictionary_of_National_Biography_1885_1900/Pitt_William_(1708–1778)> p. 355.

77. See Christopher Duffy, *The '45: Bonnie Prince Charlie and the Untold Story of the Jacobite Rising* (London: Weidenfeld & Nicolson, 2007).

78. 'March of the Guards to Finchley', <ww.foundlingmuseum.org.uk> (2019).

79. Jesse, *Memoirs of the Court of England*, vol. 3, p. 32. George Augustus somewhat spoiled the effect by adding melodramatically, 'I am resolved to die King of England.'

80. See John Prebble, *Culloden* (1961; London: Pimlico, 2002).

81. <en.wikipedia.org/wiki/The_Skye_Boat_Song> (2017).

82. Almon, *Review*, p. 91.

83. 'Bonnie Charlie's noo awa' ('Will ye no come back again?'), poem by Caroline Oliphant, published 1869.

84. *The Literary World*, vol. 13 (London, 1876), p. 100.

85. Randall Lesaffer, 'The Treaty of Aachen', *Oxford Public International Law*, <opil.ouplaw.com/page/559.> (2020).

86. Robert Wilde 'The Diplomatic Revolution of 1756', <thoughtco.com/the-diplomatic-revolution-1756–1222017> (2020).

87. The king-elector's electoral ministers certainly took notice. All of them had grown up knowing that the Electorate formed part of the Holy Roman Empire and assuming that loyalty to the Empire was the norm. Most of them had always been strongly anti-Prussian, and were aghast at the very idea of a Prussian alliance. Their dismay led to early discussions about the future of the Electorate's union with Great Britain. See Thompson, *George II*, chapter 9, 'Ultimate Victory?', p. 255 ff.

88. See Daniel Marston, *The Seven Years' War* (Oxford: Osprey, 2001).

89. Andrew Thompson, 'William Pitt the Elder', <history.blog.gov.uk/2015/03/11/William-pitt-the-elder-whig-1766–1768> (2020).

90. J. W. von Archenholtz, *Histoire de la guerre de Sept Ans en Allemagne, de 1756 à 1763* (Metz, 1789), pp. 62–3.

91. Ibid., p. 77.

92. 'Hearts [or Heart] of Oak', words by David Garrick, music by William Boyce.

93. W. T. Waugh, *James Wolfe: Man and Soldier* (Montreal: Louis Carrier, 1928).

94. See Michael Scott, *Scapegoats: Thirteen Victims of Military Injustice* (London: Elliott & Thompson, 2013).

95. See <quoteinvestigator.com/2013/01/15/bite-my-generals> (2020).

8. DUSK

1. As in the last portrait by Thomas Worlidge painted in 1753, when he wore a brocaded waistcoat under a soft velvet jacket with wide sleeves (National Portrait Gallery, 256). George Augustus also liked to dress up in his old uniform from Oudenarde and to listen to the recital of poems from that period. Jesse, *Memoirs of the Court of England*, vol. 3, p. 36.

2. Horace Walpole, 1756 quoted by R. W. Ketton-Cremer, *Horace Walpole: A Biography* (London: Methuen, 1964), p. 127.

3. See John Hervey, Baron Hervey, *Memoirs of the Reign of George the Second, from his accession to the death of Queen Caroline* (London, 1848).

4. Eliot Warburton (ed.), *Memoirs of Horace Walpole and His Contemporaries* (London, 1852, 2 vols); Horace Walpole, *Memoirs of King George II* (New Haven, CT and London: Yale University Press, 1985); W. S. Lewis (ed.), *The Yale Edition of Horace Walpole's Correspondence* (New Haven, CT: Yale University Press, 1937–83, 48 vols). See also Mrs A. T. Thomson, *Memoirs of the Court and Times of King George the Second and his Consort, Queen Caroline* (London, 1850, 2 vols).

5. See Timothy Mowl, *Horace Walpole: The Great Outsider* (London: Faber & Faber, 2011), Introduction.

6. The visit of 1755, the twelfth since 1727, was to be the king-elector's last. See Thompson, *George II*, pp. 86–90. Discounting the years when travel was impossible, the average works out at one visit every other year. The monarch usually left London in July during the parliamentary recess and returned in late October for his birthday. This was no holiday, but the time when he could concentrate on governing the Electorate.

7. When staying at Herrenhausen, George Augustus occupied a modest suite of rooms at the end of the east wing, which had direct access to the garden. The grander state apartments on the first floor of the central block were reserved for formal occasions. See Adam, 'Herrenhausen', p. 25.

8. This version of the words may be anachronistic for 1755, though there can be no doubt that this or some other similar version was already current. See <koenigreich-hannover.de/ukindex2.html> (2019).

9. Thanks to the departure of Hanbury Williams, Britain had no ambassador in Prussia and Prussia none in London, and the Convention was signed by the secretary of legation, Louis Michell, a Swiss, who wasn't even a Prussian citizen. See Patrick F. Doran, *Andrew Mitchell and Anglo-Prussian Diplomatic Relations during the Seven Years War* (Abingdon: Routledge, 2020), chapter 2, 'Genesis of an Entente'.

10. Over 2,000 tons deadweight. Twenty-six years later, in 1782, the *Royal George* was to sink at its moorings off Portsmouth, causing one of the Royal Navy's greatest maritime disasters. See Hilary Rubinstein, *Catastrophe at Spithead: The Sinking of the Royal George* (Barnsley: Seaforth, 2020).

11. https://archive.org/royalproclamations12brigrich/_jvu.txt (2019).

12. Jesse, *Memoirs of the Court of England*, vol. 3, p. 23.

13. See *A Country Parson: James Woodforde's Diary 1759–1802* (London: Century, 1985).

14. Thompson, *George II*, pp. 210–13, 270–71.

9. DECEASE

1. *Gentleman's Magazine*, vol. 30 (1760), p. 38.

2. 'In Story We're Told', Thompson, *George II*, pp. 286–7.

3. Minden, <britishbattles.com/seven-years-war/battle-of-minden> (2020).

4. Robert Frost comments: 'The Welfs coped admirably with the problems of a composite monarchy. The Wettins did not.' 'Some Hidden Thunder', p. 211. The Hesse-Kassels had already lost their Swedish throne in 1751.

5. *London Gazette*, 26 April 1760, quoted by J. Entick, *The General History of the Late War* (London, 1763), vol. 4, pp. 81–2.

6. Ibid.

7. *Gentleman's Magazine*, vol. 30 (1760), p. 136.

8. Laurence Shirley, 4th Earl Ferrers (1720–60), a cousin of Selina, Countess of Huntingdon, was convicted after pleading insanity, and hanged in his wedding suit. His earldom passed to his younger brother, Washington Shirley (1722–78), Grand Master of the Premier Freemasons' Lodge and soon to be vice-admiral RN.

9. See *Stowe*, Stowe House brochure, n.d. (*c*.2018).

10. 9–12 October 1760: 'Russian Troops take Berlin during the Seven Years' War', <prlib.ru/en/history/619614> (2020). The king-elector would probably have heard of the Russians' withdrawal from Berlin after three days, together with a ransom of 1,500,000 *Thaler*, but not of the arrest of the commander of the Russian forces, General Gottlob-Heinrich Curt von Tottleben (1715–73), on charges of 'spying'.

11. *Gentleman's Magazine*, vol. 30 (1760), pp. 485–6.

12. Ibid.

13. Fiona Callaghan, 'Dissecting a King', <blogs.royalsociety.org/history-of-science/2020/02/11/dissecting-a-king>; Franks Nicholls, FRS, 'Concerning the post-mortem examination of the body of the late king', Royal Society, *Philosophical Transactions*, vol. 52 (1762), with illustration, tab. 12, p. 274.

14. Borman, *King's Mistress*, p. 267.

10. LEGACY

1. All the money came from electoral funds. Cumberland's bequest included the instruction to care for his unmarried sisters. Amelia and Caroline (who had died in the meantime) were allotted 65,000 *Thaler* each, the Countess of Yarmouth 100,000, and the Hanoverian officials 25,000 between them. Prince George was to receive the king-elector's jewels. Thompson, *George II*, pp. 211–12.

2. Amounting to about £8,000 – three-quarters in paper money, and one quarter in coin. Jesse, *Memoirs of the Court of England*, vol. 3, *passim*. The Countess of Yarmouth could

have carried off the paper money, presumably in banknotes and bills of exchange, but not the heavy coins (without a trolley): £2,000 in 381 five-guinea pieces would have weighed about 16 kilos.

3. *Gentleman's Magazine*, vol. 30 (1760), p. 486.

4. See Matthias Range, *British Royal and State Funerals: Music and Ceremonial since Elizabeth* I (Woodbridge: Boydell Press, 2016).

5. Ibid., pp. 540–41.

6. Walpole, *Memoirs*, vol. 1, p. 175.

7. Ibid., p. 180.

8. Quoted by Chenevix-Trench, *George II*, p. 270.

9. Ibid., p. 269.

10. Ibid., p. 301.

11. Ibid., p. 299.

12. Almon, *Review*, p. 254ff.

13. See Herbert Butterfield, *The Whig Interpretation of History* (1931; Harmondsworth: Penguin, 1973).

14. Worsley, 'Why do the Georgians matter?'; see Chapter 3, note 12.

15. Worsley, ibid., commenting on the *Horrible Histories* book series, 1993–2013.

16. See W. C. Sellar and R. J. Yeatman, *1066 and All That* (London: Methuen, 1930).

17. *Encyclopaedia Britannica* (11th edn, 1912), vol. 11, pp. 638–9.

18. J. H. Plumb in *The First Four Georges* (London: Batsford, 1956).

19. Harry T. Dickinson, in *Walpole and the Whig Supremacy* (London: English Universities Press, 1973).

20. Walter Savage Landor, 'The Georges': <poemhunter.com/the-georges> (2020). The verse continues: 'And what mortal ever heard / Any good of George the Third. / And from the earth the Fourth descended. / God be praised the Georges ended./

21. Chenevix-Trench, *George II*, p. 299.

22. Thompson concludes: 'George was not a figurehead monarch . . . [but] the ultimate "man of business" in both Britain and Hanover.' *George II*, p. 296.

23. Thomas Gray, 'Elegy Written in a Country Churchyard' (1751), lines 37–40.

Further Reading

COMPOSITE STATES/COMPOSITE MONARCHIES

The concept of composite states or monarchies has been familiar to historians of early modern Europe for over forty years, and is reg_ularly applied to the histories of Spain, Austria and even France. It has sometimes been invoked in relation to seventeenth-century arrangements in the British Isles, but rarely to the set-up created by the accession of the Hanoverian Guelphs in 1714. The subject of this biography, therefore, who ruled for thirty-three years over 'Great Britain-Hanover', could be a central figure in determining the international, compound nature of early Georgian statehood.

J. H. Elliott, 'A Europe of Composite Monarchies', *Past and Present*, vol. 137 (1992), pp. 48–71.

Robert Frost, ' "Some Hidden Thunder": Hanover, Saxony and the Management of the Political Union, 1697–1763', in B. S. Sirota and A. I. Macinnes (eds), *The Hanoverian Succession in Great Britain and its Empire* (Martlesham: Boydell & Brewer, 2019), pp.193–211.

D. Hayton, J. Kelly and J. Bergin (eds), *The Eighteenth-century Composite State: Representative Institutions in Ireland and Europe, 1689–1800* (Basingstoke: Palgrave Macmillan, 2010).

H. G. Koenigsberger, 'Monarchies and Parliaments in Early Modern Europe', *Theory and Society*, vol. 5(2) (1978), pp. 191–219.

THE HOLY ROMAN EMPIRE

Although George Augustus broke faith with the Holy Roman Empire towards the end of his reign, he remained a lifelong imperial subject and, as prince-elector, a vassal of the emperor. From his perspective, therefore, and that of his monarchy, the Empire provided more than mere background or an object of foreign policy: it was an integral part of the world that surrounded him and his realms.

R. J. W. Evans, *The Making of the Habsburg Monarchy, 1550–1700: An Interpretation* (Oxford: Oxford University Press, 2000).

Pieter Judson, *The Habsburg Empire: A New History* (Cambridge, MA and London: Harvard University Press, 2016).

Martyn Rady, *The Habsburgs: The Rise and Fall of a World Power* (London: Allen Lane, 2020).

FRANCE

As Europe's leading power, the France of Louis XIV and XV loomed large throughout the life of George Augustus. Whilst speaking French by preference, and displaying the French lilies on his coat of arms, he was very aware that the fear of France provided the strongest cement for binding together the union of Great Britain-Hanover.

William Doyle (ed.), *The Oxford Handbook of the Ancien Régime* (Oxford: Oxford University Press, 2011).

Emmanuel LeRoy Ladurie (trans. Mark Greenglass), *The Ancien Regime: A History of France, 1610–1774* (Oxford: Blackwell, 1996).

Jeremy Black, *Natural and Necessary Enemies: Anglo-French Relations in the Eighteenth Century* (London: Duckworth, 1986).

THE ELECTORATE

George Augustus's homeland, the Electorate of Brunswick-Lüneburg, the *Kurfürstentum Hannover*, was tied by personal union to Great

Britain and Ireland for 106 years. (Prior to its abolition in 1806 as part of the Holy Roman Empire, it was nominally tied for five years to the United Kingdom, though occupied by foreign forces.) Reconstituted in 1814 as a hereditary kingdom, it was reunited with Britain for twenty-three years more. To understand how the relationship between Britain and Hanover evolved, one needs to examine it at different phases of its existence. The reign of George Augustus belongs to the middle period.

A. M. Birke and Kurt Kluxen (eds), *England und Hannover/England and Hanover* (Munich: K. G. Sauer, 1986).

Tim Blanning, '"That Horrid Electorate" or "Ma Patrie germanique"? George III, Hanover and the Fürstenbund of 1785', *Historical Journal* 20 (1977), pp. 311–44.

Harding, Nick, *Hanover and the British Empire, 1700–1837* (Woodbridge: Boydell Press, 2006).

Heide Rohloff (ed.), *Grossbritannien und Hannover. Die Zeit der Personalunion, 1714–1837* (Frankfurt/Main: Fischer, 1989).

Brendan Simms and Torsten Riotte (eds), *The Hanoverian Dimension in British History, 1714–1837* (Cambridge: Cambridge University Press, 2007).

THE EARLY BRITISH STATE: PARLIAMENT AND MONARCHY

In the English tradition of statehood, the idea of continuity is paramount and the significance of changes brought about by successive unions, in 1707 and 1714, is underplayed. As a result, the power of Parliament vis-à-vis the monarchy, as established in late Stuart England, is often assumed to have continued unaltered into the Georgian period. This was not necessarily the case.

The Georgian Papers Programme is an ongoing, ambitious online project which is mining the Royal Archives and Royal Collection as sources of new information on the period 1714–1820. See <georgian-papers.com>.

Brian Hill, 'Executive monarchy and the challenge of parties: Two concepts of government and two historiographical interpretations', *Historical Journal*, vol. 13 (1970), pp. 379–401. Published online by Cambridge University Press.

Lewis Namier, *The Structure of Politics at the Accession of George III* (London: Macmillan, 1929).

Hannah Smith, *Georgian Monarchy: Politics and Culture, 1714–60* (Cambridge: Cambridge University Press, 2006).

W. A. Speck, *Stability and Strife: England, 1714–60* (London: Edward Arnold, 1977).

GREAT BRITAIN AND IRELAND

George Augustus embodied a personal union which saw England joined to Scotland in the Kingdom of Great Britain, and Ireland ruled as an English dependency. This configuration differed from constitutional arrangements before 1707 and after 1801, and must be carefully considered if the position of the monarch within in it, and of the various categories of his subjects, is to be properly gauged.

Linda Colley, *Britons: Forging the Nation, 1707–1837* (New Haven, CT and London: Yale University Press, 1992).

M. Fry, *The Union: England, Scotland and the Treaty of 1707* (Edinburgh: Birlinn, 2006).

T. W. Moody and W. F. Vaughan (eds), *A New History of Ireland*, vol. 4: *Eighteenth-century Ireland, 1691–1800* (Oxford: Oxford University Press, 1986).

THE HANOVERIAN GUELPHS

The ruling dynasty, known to the British as the Hanoverians, possessed a corporate identity which, as their coat of arms displays, was not limited to the British part of their inheritance. The extent of their commitments in Germany was poorly understood by their original English hosts, and their sense of Britishness remained relatively weak until after 1760. In George Augustus's time the dynasty's authority was undisputed in the Electorate, but up to 1745 was repeatedly contested by the Stuarts' Jacobite supporters.

Jeremy Black, *The Hanoverians: The History of a Dynasty* (London: Bloomsbury, 2004).

John Prebble, *Culloden* (Harmondsworth: Penguin, 1967).

BIOGRAPHIES

It has been the work of decades for biographers to rescue George Augustus from the neglect and undeserved disrepute into which he had fallen. Most recently, the undervalued monarch has been restored to his rightful dignity as both 'king' and 'elector', but the twin sides of his rule and personality, German and British, still await full exposition.

Jeremy Black, *George II: Puppet of the Politicians?* (Exeter: University of Exeter Press, 2007).

Charles Chenevix-Trench, *George II* (London: Allen Lane, 1973).

Andrew Thompson, *George II: King and Elector* (New Haven, CT and London: Yale University Press, 2011).

CONTEMPORARIES

It is natural for a monarch to be compared to his predecessors, but to understand the predicament and outlook of George Augustus one also needs to imagine how he thought of himself. In particular, it makes good sense to compare him with his peers and contemporaries, especially with other continental 'warrior princes' of the age.

Tim Blanning, *Frederick the Great, King of Prussia* (London: Allen Lane, 2015).

Tim Blanning, *George I: The Lucky King* (London: Allen Lane, 2017).

Tony Claydon, *William III* (Harlow: Longman, 2002).

Ragnhild Hatton, *Charles XII of Sweden* (London: Historical Association, 1974).

G. F. MacMunn, *Prince Eugene: Twin Marshal with Marlborough* (London: Sampson Low & Co., 1934).

John Manchip White, *Marshal of France: The Life and Times of Maurice, Comte de Saxe, 1696–1750* (London: Hamish Hamilton, 1962). As George Augustus well knew, the great Field Marshal de Saxe was the nephew of his mother's murdered lover, Count Königsmarck.

Charles Petrie, *King Charles III of Spain: An Enlightened Despot* (London: Constable, 1971).

Gerhard Ritter (trans Peter Paret), *Frederick the Great: A Historical Profile* (Berkeley, CA: University of California Press, 1968).

Tony Sharp, *Pleasure and Ambition: The Life, Loves and Wars of Augustus the Strong* (London: I. B. Tauris, 2001).

Picture Credits

PICTURE CREDITS

24. Augustus II of Poland by Nicolas de Largillierre, *c.* 1714 (Wikimedia Commons CC BY-SA 3.0)

25. *The Victorious Charge of the Irish Brigade at Fontenoy*, 1745, coloured lithograph *c.* 1840 (courtesy of Adams Auctioneers, Dublin)

26. *The 'Royal George' at Deptford showing the launch of 'The Cambridge'*. The painting purports to show HMS *Royal George* (*right*) standing by as HMS *Cambridge*, a lesser, third-rate vessel, of 80 guns, was launched. In reality, the scene could not have happened: the *Cambridge* was launched at Deptford in 1755, one year before construction of the *Royal George* was completed. (© National Maritime Museum, Greenwich, London)

Index